GW00995268

How to access your on-line resources

Kaplan Financial students will have a MyKaplan account and these extra resources will be available to you online. You do not need to register again, as this process was completed when you enrolled. If you are having problems accessing online materials, please ask your course administrator.

If you are not studying with Kaplan and did not purchase your book via a Kaplan website, to unlock your extra online resources please go to www.en-gage.co.uk (even if you have set up an account and registered books previously). You will then need to enter the ISBN number (on the title page and back cover) and the unique pass key number contained in the scratch panel below to gain access.

You will also be required to enter additional information during this process to set up or confirm your account details.

If you purchased via the Kaplan Publishing website you will automatically receive an e-mail invitation to register your details and gain access to your content. If you do not receive the e-mail or book content, please contact Kaplan Publishing.

Your code and information

This code can only be used once for the registration of one book online. This registration and your online content will expire when the final sittings for the examinations covered by this book have taken place. Please allow one hour from the time you submit your book details for us to process your request.

Please scratch the film to access your unique code.

Please be aware that this code is case-sensitive and you will need to include the dashes within the passcode, but not when entering the ISBN.

CIMA

Case Study

Strategic Level

Study Text

Published by: Kaplan Publishing UK

Unit 2 The Business Centre, Molly Millars Lane, Wokingham, Berkshire RG41 2QZ

Acknowledgements

We are grateful to the CIMA for permission to reproduce past examination questions and the official CIMA answers.

Notice

British Library Cataloguing in Publication Data

A catalogue record for this book is available from the British Library.

ISBN: 978-1-78740-204-1

Printed and bound in Great Britain

Contents

Introduction

Acknowledgements

Every effort has been made to contact the holders of copyright material, but if any here have been inadvertently overlooked the publishers will be pleased to make the necessary arrangements at the first opportunity.

How to use the Materials

 Test your understanding – Following key points and definitions are exercises which give the opportunity to assess the understanding of these core areas. Within the work book the answers to these sections are left blank, explanations to the questions can be found within the online version which can be hidden or shown on screen to enable repetition of activities.

 Illustration – to help develop an understanding of topics and the test your understanding exercises the illustrative examples can be used.

Quality and accuracy are of the utmost importance to us so if you spot an error in any of our products, please send an email to mykaplanreporting@kaplan.com with full details.

Our Quality Coordinator will work with our technical team to verify the error and take action to ensure it is corrected in future editions.

Exam Introduction

To complete the CIMA qualification and be able to use the designatory letters of ACMA and CGMA, candidates for this prestigious award need to achieve three things:

- attain the entry requirements for the professional level qualification
- study for and complete the relevant professional level assessments and examinations
- complete three years of relevant practical experience

This text concentrates on the second of these requirements, and in particular to study for and complete the Strategic level case study exam.

Overview of exam

The case study exam will be available four times a year. The purpose of this exam is to consolidate learning at each level by reflecting real life work situations. The exam is human marked.

This approach allows a wide range of knowledge and skills to be tested including research and analysis, presentation of information and communication skills whilst still ensuring competence in key skills.

CIMA believe that this format will provide the commitment to delivering the competencies which employers desire thereby improving 'employability'.

For example, the Strategic level case study exam will be set within a simulated business context, placing the candidate in the job role matched to the competency level. In the case of the Strategic level, the job role is that of a senior finance manager, reporting to the highest levels of management within the organisation. The focus will be on the long-term, involving the strategic direction of the organisation.

The exam is intended to replicate "a day in the life" of a finance professional operating at the strategic level and provide a simulated environment for candidates to demonstrate the required level of proficiency in each of the competency areas. Consequently, the exam will be set and marked according to the weightings for each core activity at the level.

The case study exam is 3 hours in duration and is made up of a series of timed tests or tasks. This makes the case study exam different from most exams you will have sat to date – once you have submitted a particular task (or the time limit is reached, whichever is sooner) you will be moved on and will not be able to return to that task. This should reduce the problem of not completing the paper but does mean you will need to be very disciplined when attempting each task.

Candidates will be provided with access to pre-seen information approximately seven weeks before the real exam.

Assessment aims and strategy

The Case Study Examination tests the knowledge, skills and techniques from the three pillars within one simulated scenario and is taken at the end of each level of the CIMA Professional Qualification. Candidates are given a fictional Case Study before the examination and are expected to give solutions to the situations and challenges presented within the examination – based on the knowledge and skills acquired from the three subjects. The Case Study mimics their role in a real-work scenario, at each level of the qualification.

The case study is three hours long. The case study will include both pre-seen and unseen material, the latter being made available during the examination. They will incorporate short written answers, emails, letters and any form of appropriate communication required within the tasks set.

The focus is on application, analysis and evaluation which are levels 3, 4 and 5 of the CIMA hierarchy of verbs (see below).

Simulated business issues in the case studies provide candidates with the opportunity to demonstrate their familiarity with the context and interrelationships of the level's technical content. This reflects the cross functional abilities required in the workplace. Skills will include research, analysis, presentation of both financial and nonfinancial information and communication skills.

Feedback will be provided to candidates with their results. Exam sittings for the case studies will occur every three months. Candidates must have completed or be exempt from the three objective tests at a particular level before attempting the relevant integrated case study.

Core activities and assessment outcomes

Within each Strategic Case Study Examination, five "core activities" will be assessed. These core activities represent the tasks that are most frequent, critical and important to the senior finance professional role.

The five core activities are:

A   Develop business strategy.

B   Evaluate the business ecosystem and business environment.

C   Recommend financing strategies.

D   Evaluate and mitigate risk.

E   Recommend and maintain a sound control environment.

The core activities are linked to associated assessment outcomes expressed in terms of 'I Can' statements that speak directly to the skills and competencies that drive the employability of successful learners.

The core activities require and draw together the knowledge, skills and techniques acquired while studying for Objective Tests and combining them with the mindset of a CIMA finance professional.

Each core activity is translated into a number of "assessment outcomes". These are a clear assertion of what a CIMA qualified finance professional should be able to do when the Examination has been completed and what the assessment will be designed to measure. Case Study assessment outcomes will be synoptic

These are discussed in more detail in chapters 1 and 2.

Assessing skills – the CIMA verb hierarchy

CIMA has adopted a skill framework for the assessments based on the revised Bloom's Taxonomy of Education Objectives. Bloom's Taxonomy classifies a continuum of skills that learners are expected to know and demonstrate.

The case study exam will focus on Levels 3, 4 and 5.

Skill level	Verbs used	Definition
Level 5 Evaluation How you are expected to use your learning to evaluate, make decisions or recommendations	Advise	Counsel, inform or notify
	Assess	Evaluate or estimate the nature, ability or quality of
	Evaluate	Appraise or assess the value of
	Recommend	Propose a course of action
	Review	Assess and evaluate in order, to change if necessary
Level 4 Analysis How you are expected to analyse the detail of what you have learned	Align	Arrange in an orderly way
	Analyse	Examine in detail the structure of
	Communicate	Share or exchange information
	Compare and contrast	Show the similarities and/or differences between
	Develop	Grow and expand a concept
	Discuss	Examine in detail by argument
	Examine	Inspect thoroughly
	Interpret	Translate into intelligible or familiar terms
	Monitor	Observe and check the progress of
	Prioritise	Place in order of priority or sequence for action
	Produce	Create or bring into existence
Level 3 Application How you are expected to apply your knowledge	Apply	Put to practical use
	Calculate	Ascertain or reckon mathematically
	Conduct	Organise and carry out
	Demonstrate	Prove with certainty or exhibit by practical means
	Prepare	Make or get ready for use
	Reconcile	Make or prove consistent/compatible
Level 2 Comprehension What you are expected to understand	Describe	Communicate the key features of
	Distinguish	Highlight the differences between
	Explain	Make clear or intelligible/state the meaning or purpose of
	Identify	Recognise, establish or select after consideration
	Illustrate	Use an example to describe or explain something
Level 1 Knowledge What you are expected to know	List	Make a list of
	State	Express, fully or clearly, the details/facts of
	Define	Give the exact meaning of
	Outline	Give a summary of

How to use the material

These Official CIMA learning materials brought to you by CIMA and Kaplan Publishing have been carefully designed to make your learning experience as easy as possible and give you the best chances of success in your Case Study Examinations.

This Study Text has been designed with the needs of home study and distance learning candidates in mind. However, the Study Text is also ideal for fully taught courses.

The aim of this textbook is to walk you through the stages to prepare for, and to answer, the requirements of the Case Study Examination.

Practical hints and realistic tips are given throughout the book making it easy for you to apply what you've learned in this text to your actual Case Study Exam.

Where sample solutions are provided, they must be viewed as just one interpretation of the case. One key aspect, which you must appreciate early in your studies, is that there is no single 'correct' solution.

Your own answer might reach different conclusions, and give greater emphasis to some issues and less emphasis to others, but score equally as well if it demonstrates the required skills.

If you work conscientiously through the official CIMA Study Text according to the guidelines above, as well as analysing the pre-seen information in full, you will be giving yourself an excellent chance of success in your examination. Good luck with your studies!

Planning

To begin with, formal planning is essential to get the best return from the time you spend studying. Estimate how much time in total you are going to need for each subject you are studying for the Case Study Examination. You may find it helpful to read "Pass First Time!" second edition by David R. Harris ISBN 978-1-85617-798-6.

This book will provide you with proven study techniques. Chapter by chapter it covers the building blocks of successful learning and examination techniques and shows you how to earn all the marks you deserve, and explains how to avoid the most common pitfalls.

With your study material before you, decide which chapters you are going to study in each week, which weeks you will devote to practising past exams, and which weeks you will spend becoming familiar with your case study pre-seen material.

Prepare a written schedule summarising the above and stick to it! Students are advised to refer to articles published regularly in CIMA's magazine (Financial Management), the student e-newsletter (Velocity) and on the CIMA website, to ensure they are up to date with relevant issues and topics.

Tips for effective studying

1   Aim to find a quiet and undisturbed location for your study, and plan as far as possible to use the same period of time each day. Getting into a routine helps to avoid wasting time. Make sure that you have all the materials you need before you begin so as to minimise interruptions.

2   Store all your materials in one place, so that you do not waste time searching for items every time you want to begin studying. If you have to pack everything away after each study period, keep your study materials in a box, or even a suitcase, which will not be disturbed until the next time.

3   Limit distractions. To make the most effective use of your study periods you should be able to apply total concentration, so turn off all entertainment equipment, set your phones to message mode, and put up your 'do not disturb' sign.

4   Your timetable will tell you which topic to study. However, before diving in and becoming engrossed in the finer points, make sure you have an overall picture of all the areas that need to be covered by the end of that session. After an hour, allow yourself a short break and move away from your Study Text. With experience, you will learn to assess the pace you need to work at. Each study session should focus on component learning outcomes – the basis for all questions.

5   Work carefully through a chapter, making notes as you go. When you have covered a suitable amount of material, vary the pattern by attempting a practice question. When you have finished your attempt, make notes of any mistakes you made, or any areas that you failed to cover or covered more briefly. Be aware that all component learning outcomes will be tested in each examination.

6   Make notes as you study, and discover the techniques that work best for you. Your notes may be in the form of lists, bullet points, diagrams, summaries, 'mind maps', or the written word, but remember that you will need to refer back to them at a later date, so they must be intelligible. If you are on a taught course, make sure you highlight any issues you would like to follow up with your lecturer.

7   Organise your notes. Make sure that all your notes, calculations etc. can be effectively filed and easily retrieved later.

Relevant practical experience

In order to become a Chartered Global Management Accountant (ACMA, CGMA), you need a minimum of three years' verified relevant work-based practical experience.

Read the 'Applying for Membership' brochure for full details of the practical experience requirements (PER).

Information concerning formulae and tables will be provided via the CIMA website, www.cimaglobal.com, and your EN-gage login.

Introduction to case study exams

Chapter learning objectives

- To gain an overview of the case study exam, its purpose, structure and the process involved.

1 The structure of the CIMA Strategic Level

Each level of CIMA's professional qualification consists of three objective test 'pillar' exams, followed by the Case Study Examination.

You can only attempt the Case Study Examination after all objective tests for the level have been completed or if exemptions have been given.

For the 2019 syllabus the three Strategic level pillar exams are as follows:

- E3 – Strategic Management
- P3 – Risk Management
- F3 – Financial Strategy

The objective tests for each of these individual subjects ensure the acquisition of the breadth of knowledge, skills and techniques that provide the foundation for approaching the Case Study Examination.

2 Why a Case Study Examination?

The CIMA Case Study Examinations are 'capstone' examinations designed to demonstrate mastery of previously acquired knowledge, skills and techniques and the drawing together of these to provide solutions to unstructured, synoptic problems.

Each synoptic assessment combines the content covered in all three pillar subjects at the level into a single assessment. Its aim is the "undoing" of the pillar and subject divisions of the syllabus and the application of knowledge, skills and techniques to the type of problems that you might encounter in the workplace in a role matched to the appropriate level of the qualification.

The examination uses a Case Study to provide a rich, immersive scenario to prepare and to provide a context for the tasks in the examination. The scenarios are developed around today's modern business environment and the challenges that you will face – allowing you to demonstrate the 'core activities' that have been identified by employers as critical.

Examination tasks will be practical and applied, not theoretical or academic. To be successful, you will have to perform these core activities in the same way and to the same standards that would be valid and valued in the workplace.

The Case Study Examination is thus an attempt to simulate workplace problem solving, and allows examiners to move one step closer to the assessment of competence than is possible with objective test questions. It is a test of both professional competence and, by implication, employability.

In addition, the purpose of the Case Study Examination is to assess your proficiency in those specific skills that are less likely to be automated.

The purpose of this text is to suggest how you might prepare for the examination by developing and practising your skills. Since the examination tests a range of different skills, preparing for this examination needs to be different from studying for a 'traditional' examination.

3 Your role

Each case study exam will be set within a simulated business context, placing the candidate in the job role matched to the competency level.

In the case of the strategic level your role is that of a senior finance manager reporting to the highest levels of management, either an individual director or the board of directors as a whole.

This role can be broken down as follows:

- A senior finance manager advising the organisation's leaders in the development of business strategy to create value is required to evaluate strategic options, paying due attention to the organisation's ecosystem. Risk management is a significant part of the overall responsibility, including cyber risks.

- There is a duty to advise on issues relating to corporate governance. They are important both because of the reputational risks arising from poor governance and the threats to the well-being of internal and external stakeholders when boards are poorly structured and badly managed. As an important element of this, the senior finance manager is frequently involved in the evaluation of the control environment and the management of internal audit. The need to manage control is crucial given the increasing dangers arising from cyber risks.

- The frequent requirement to support strategic decision-making may require the formulation of models and other methods of justifying and legitimating decisions. The senior finance manager is also involved in the raising of finance from suitable sources in order to ensure that new strategic projects are adequately resourced.

- The business case for digitisation and the manner in which the entity creates partnerships for ensuring strategic success must be understood, as must the operation of capital markets in determining value.

- The senior finance manager advises on matters that involve considerable judgement and that may have a significant effect on stakeholders and therefore must adhere to high standards of professionalism and ethics in the course of their duties.

In summary, the Strategic level focuses on the long term and the identification, evaluating and implementation of successful strategies. The Strategic Case Study examination expects the learner to think and respond like a senior finance manager.

4   The exam 'blueprints'

For the first time, CIMA has released blueprints for its Professional Qualification Examination. The intent is that blueprints will demystify the examination — giving greater clarity on examinable topics; assessment approach, design and weightings; and learner expectations.

The Case Study Examination blueprint contains the following:

- **Core activities** – Business-related tasks that are common to the role being simulated and valued by employers which, if performed satisfactorily, enables the demonstration of the assessment outcomes.

- **Assessment outcomes** – A clear assertion of what a CIMA qualified finance professional can do when the Examination has been completed and what the assessment will be designed to measure. Case Study assessment outcomes will be synoptic.

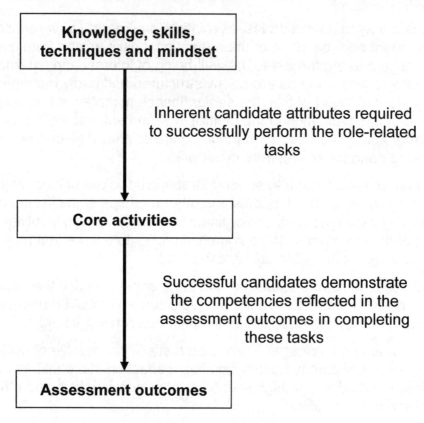

All core activities will be assessed in each form of the examination in line with the weightings. A sample of related assessment outcomes will be tested.

Blueprints are discussed in more detail in chapter 2.

5 The exam process

5.1 Overview

The examination is three hours long. A 15-minute tutorial is available before the start of the examination to allow candidates to familiarise themselves with the test driver.

The examination has three sections (tasks), which are each 1 hour long. All sections are equally weighted. Candidates may finish a section early and move on to the next but cannot return to previous sections in the time remaining.

There may be more than one sub-task within each section and an indication of how long to spend on each sub-task will be given to allow candidates to manage their time. If no weighting is given, then candidates should assume that the sub-tasks are equally weighted.

For example, the first exam variant of the sample prototype paper shows the following instructions:

Section (task)	Time for section (minutes)	Number of answer screens	Number of sub-tasks	% time to spend on each sub-task
1	60	1	2	(a) 55% (b) 45%
2	60	1	2	(a) 55% (b) 45%
3	60	1	3	(a) 60% (b) 20% (c) 20%

More than one core activity will normally (but not always) be assessed in each section/task and the order of core activities and assessment outcomes in the blueprint does not reflect how these might be structured in the examination.

For each sitting there are a number of variants, so different students will not necessarily face the same exam tasks. You are not permitted to discuss any aspects of the variant you sat until after the exam window has finished. The marking and moderation processes ensure that no advantage is gained from sitting one particular variant rather than another.

5.2 The pre-seen

The exam is based on:

- pre-seen material issued in advance of the exam day, supplemented by

- additional, previously unseen material given to you in the exam room.

From the May 2020 sitting onwards, one pre-seen will be used over two exam windows, giving candidates the opportunity to resit using the same pre-seen. The pre-seen will be shared as follows:

- May / August

- November / February

CIMA releases the pre-seen material approximately seven weeks before the first examination. This is posted on the student area of the CIMA website (www.cimaglobal.com) and it is your responsibility to download it and to print off a copy.

The pre-seen material is an introductory scenario to set the scene for the case study, together with accounting and financial information. The pre-seen material is an extended scenario consisting of approximately ten exhibits giving information about a business organisation.

You will be taking on the role of a management accountant who works for the organisation, and your responses to the tasks will usually be addressed to your superior.

5.3 The unseen

In the examination you will be provided with the following.

- An on-screen version of the pre-seen material

- Additional new unseen material, which contains both triggers (new information) and tasks (what you need to do)

- Space to complete your answers

- An on-screen calculator (although candidates are permitted to take their own calculators as long as it's a CIMA approved model.)

- Reference materials (Present value tables, Cumulative present value tables and Normal distribution tables)

- A notepad and pen for planning and workings along with an on-screen scratch pad.

The unseen material will be a continuation of the pre-seen and will usually bring the scenario up to date. In many cases there is a 'twist' in the unseen i.e. a development that students might not have anticipated from the pre-seen. The unseen may focus on a number of issues that appeared in the pre-seen or it may just focus on one or two; either way it will provide the basis for the content of your answers.

A common mistake made by weaker students is that they place too much emphasis on their analysis of the pre-seen material and do not develop the information in the unseen material adequately. The key points to be referred to in your answer should be driven by the new information in the unseen material.

5.4 Triggers and tasks

Each section in the unseen material will begin with a **trigger.**

This will be information provided as an introduction to the work that you are required to complete.

The information may be in the form of a briefing by your superior, a newspaper article, some financial information or extracts from internal reports. You will be expected to integrate this new information with the analysis you have performed on the pre-seen material to produce a coherent and well informed response.

Within each section of the examination, there will then be a **task** or tasks that you will be asked to perform, usually by your superior. These tasks will require different types of response, although usually reports, briefing notes and emails.

Word processing capabilities will be provided within the test driver to allow the formatting and presentation of responses in a professional manner. From 2019, this includes the ability to use tables to put together a response. For full details of the word processing functionality and to try this in advance of the examination, a tutorial is available on cimaglobal.com.

There is a time limit attached to each task and you will have a clock showing the time remaining in the corner of your screen. Once you have submitted a task (or the time limit is reached, whichever is sooner) you will not be able to return to that task. This should reduce the problem of not completing the paper but does mean you will need to be disciplined when attempting each task.

If you feel that you do not need all of the time on an earlier task, then moving forwards prematurely will not allow you extra time on later tasks – the extra time will be lost. Given this, it is always advisable to use the full time allocated to each task to recheck that you have answered the question requirement in full and that you have related your response to the specific context of the case.

A walkthrough of the prototype sample exam will be carried out in chapters 3 to 5.

5.5 Calculations

Examination tasks will not be set that require specific calculations.

However, candidates should, wherever possible, show how they have used and interpreted data from the pre-seen and the new information presented during the examination and/or undertook analysis or calculations to support their responses.

6 Marking

6.1 Overview

The Case Study Examinations are human marked. The Case Study results will contain the following information:

- Grade: Pass or fail
- Scaled score: 0 to 150 with 80 and above being a pass

There is no requirement to obtain a pass or meet a minimum threshold for each core activity.

Feedback on performance against each core activity will be provided so that learners know their areas of weakness for further study.

Grade descriptors for both the overall passing standard as well as each core activity will also be released.

6.2 The 'marginally competent' student

During 2016 CIMA disclosed further information on how the pass mark is set and the importance of identifying the 'marginally competent' candidate.

The process

A detailed process was revealed that involves the following:

(1) A panel of experts debates the tasks within a variant to decide what should be expected from a student deemed competent for this task. This debate does not focus on a perfect answer but, instead, asks what would be expected of a CIMA student (or member) in practice – what is the minimum expected if we were considering employing them, for example.

(2) A sample of student scripts is then discussed and the scripts ranked. This is repeated and refined until the "marginally competent student" is identified. This student deserves to pass (but only just!) as they would be employable and have the skills expected of a CIMA student or member in the real world.

(3) The marks earned by this script are then used to set the pass mark and standardise the overall marking system. This ensures that students are not disadvantaged if they sit a "harder" variant.

In short, candidates should be reassured that CIMA goes to great lengths to ensure that there is no advantage or disadvantage to sitting one variant rather than another.

The lessons to be learned

When answering a task in the exam, you should take the same approach as if the exam was part of a job interview and ask yourself what would be required to get the job.

Your employer would be less impressed by you showing off knowledge but much more impressed that you can answer a question asked, apply your comments to the company's specific circumstances and make practical, relevant suggestions. Make sure your answers do this!

7   Summary

You should now have a basic understanding of how the case study works. All of the ideas presented in this chapter will be developed further in the remainder of this textbook.

Next steps:

(1)   It is a good idea to register with Pearson Vue to see the online version of the Question Tutorial exam as this will allow you become more familiar with the look and feel of the exam. All the relevant material from the Question Tutorial exam has been reproduced in this textbook but it is important to recognise that the CIMA case study examinations are dynamic and shouldn't be viewed as equivalent to a static paper exam.

(2)   Think about the date on which you will sit the exam and work backwards to create a sensible and achievable study timetable.

(3)   You need to ensure that your technical knowledge is up to date / full especially if the OTQ exams were sat a while ago.

It might be worth locating and gathering together any materials you already have from the supporting technical subjects (E3, P3 and F3). We will show you in later chapters how you may need to use these materials.

Core activities and assessment outcomes

Chapter learning objectives

- To understand the core activities and assessment outcomes required for the case study exam.

1   Core Activities

In some respects one could argue that everything covered in E3, F3 and P3 was still relevant for the Case Study Examination. However, to make such a daunting proposition more accessible and clear, the blueprint defines the following core activities:

	Core Activity	Weighting
A	Develop business strategy.	15 – 25%
B	Evaluate the business ecosystem and business environment.	15 – 25%
C	Recommend financing strategies.	15 – 25%
D	Evaluate and mitigate risk.	15 – 25%
E	Recommend and maintain a sound control environment.	15 – 25%

As stated in chapter 1, **all** core activities will be assessed in each form of the examination in line with the weightings.

These core activities are linked to associated assessment outcomes expressed in terms of 'I Can' statements that speak directly to the skills and competencies that drive the employability of successful learners.

At first sight it may seem that core activities A and B are driven mainly by E3 knowledge and activities, C by F3 and D and E by P3. However, for a proper understanding of how the different technical papers might be assessed in the core activities, attention must be paid to the accompanying assessment outcomes.

2 Assessment outcomes

Assessment outcomes translate core activities into a range of "I can" statements that, in case study, effectively give you the basis of the wordings for exam tasks.

Given this, it is vital that you look at the assessment outcomes and make sure you feel confident that you could answer a task worded in this way. The full list is as follows:

	Core Activities	Assessment outcomes
A	Develop business strategy.	I can evaluate strategic options (digital and otherwise).
		I can recommend strategic decisions (digital and otherwise).
		I can evaluate potential acquisitions and divestment opportunities.
		I can recommend responses to opportunities and threats arising from digital technologies.
B	Evaluate business ecosystem and business environment.	I can select and apply suitable strategic analytical tools.
		I can conduct an analysis of stakeholder needs and recommend appropriate responses.
		I can recommend appropriate responses to changes in the business ecosystem.
		I can recommend KPIs that encourage sound strategic management. I can recommend responses to economic, political and currency risks.
C	Recommend financing strategies.	I can recommend suitable sources of finance.
		I can recommend dividend policy.
		I can recommend and apply business valuation models.
D	Evaluate and mitigate risk.	I can evaluate risks and recommend responses and can maintain the corporate risk register.
		I can identify ethical dilemmas and recommend suitable responses. I can evaluate and mitigate cyber risks.
		I can recommend internal controls.

E	Recommend and maintain a sound control environment.	I can apply internal audit resources.
		I can recommend appropriate controls and evaluate the implications of compliance failures.
		I can recommend responses to the threats arising from poor governance.

In the next section we will look at how these have been examined in the real exam. Given the syllabus changes in 2019, some tasks in past exams are no longer relevant, so we have focussed on ones that are still indicative of what you might face in your exam.

3 Examples of tasks from the May 2019 exam.

3.1 Summary of pre-seen scenario

To fully appreciate examples from recent real exams it is necessary to have a basic understanding of the case.

The pre-seen for the May 2019 Strategic Case Study involves a company called Denby Healthcare. It is the second-largest private hospital group in Keeland, and reports in K$.

Industry background

Keeland is an economically developed country with high employment levels. The provision of healthcare is state-funded, with hospitals and GP surgeries paid for out of taxes. Despite a large proportion of overall state revenues being spent on healthcare, demand still outstrips supply, and hospitals struggle to meet demand. This is because of 3 principal factors:

1   Advances in preventive medicine resulting from research. This means that more time and investment is needed for diagnosis, consultations, testing, and discussing results;

2   Increased life expectancy and an ageing population;

3   Lack of alternative providers in respect of critical care services for the extremely ill.

Waiting times are a key expectation, and the Keeland government has made it mandatory that all referrals for public hospital treatment will be completed within 15 weeks.

In addition to public hospitals, there are also a number of private hospitals in Keeland. People are prepared to go private for a number of reasons: convenience (shorter waiting times and more flexibility over timing of appointments); availability of treatments (private hospitals may have more advanced equipment, or offer services that the state will not pay for, such as certain cosmetic surgeries); comfort (rooms and food are often of higher quality in private hospitals); and, for foreign patients, because Keeland offers better healthcare than is available at home.

Private hospitals do not offer all the services that public hospitals do. For example, there are no Accident & Emergency (A&E) services in the private sector, nor is there intensive care. A&E is too expensive to operate, and there is no demand for intensive care in the private sector as the public hospitals would see to such patients immediately.

There are 3 private hospital groups in Keeland, all of which offer similar standards of care and healthcare services: Bronty Health is the largest with 48 hospitals; then Denby, with 43 hospitals; and thirdly Postar Primary Care, with 32. These are the only full-scale private hospitals, and each has a presence throughout Keeland.

They each derive revenue from 4 key sources:

1   From insurance companies, who refer patients under private health schemes

2   Self-pay (Keeland) i.e. from Keeland residents who choose to pay for private healthcare

3   Foreign patients i.e. from non-Keeland residents who choose Keeland for better healthcare than they can get at home

4   KHS patients. This is where the Keeland Health Service (KHS) refers patients to private hospitals in order to meet the maximum waiting period of 15 weeks imposed by the government. The KHS pays the private hospital charges for such patients.

Professional staff consists of senior doctors, junior doctors and nurses. Senior doctors work for both the KHS and also private hospitals, with part time contracts of employment with each. Junior doctors and nurses are full-time employees of their chosen hospitals.

Denby Healthcare

Denby was founded in the early 1980s by several senior doctors, all of whom have subsequently retired. The company achieved listed status in the 1990s. Denby has grown to have 43 hospitals and 23,500 staff; this has been by both organic means and also taking over smaller hospitals.

Denby's strategy is based on achieving and maintaining a reputation for clinical excellence. Staffing is the most important element of patient care, and so the company looks to attract and motivate the best employees.

It also seeks to maximise revenues earned from KHS hospital referrals. This can only be achieved if the quality of healthcare provided by Denby meets expectation, and also if Denby is able to meet the cost and flexibility expectations of KHS hospitals.

Profit margins in private hospitals can be considerable. An example is given of a hip replacement operation, on which the mark up on total cost amounts to 89%. Different prices may be quoted to patients based on their personal circumstances – for example, if a particular patient is expected to require a longer than average stay in hospital after the operation, they will be quoted a higher price.

Denby maintains a risk register, and 5 key risks are highlighted: changing economic environment (in times of recession, unemployment increases and so there are less people covered by private health insurance); competition (there are 2 large competitors in Keeland); staffing (providing clinical excellence requires experienced and competent staff); clinical risk (i.e. the potential damage to reputation of clinical negligence); and political risk (a change in government policy may see revenue from KHS referrals decline).

Financial information

Denby has enjoyed growth in revenue of 6.4% in 2018, although income from both foreign and KHS referrals both declined compared to 2017. Operating profit grew by 35.8%. The group paid a dividend of K$23m in respect of 2018, which represented 57.5% of that year's earnings.

At the latest year end, 31 December 2018, Denby had $93m of cash and a gearing ratio (defined as debt/debt+equity) of 32.5%.

Comparable information is given for the market leader, Bronty Health Group, in the form of its latest financial statements, enabling a detailed comparison of the 2 companies' financial performance and position.

A share price graph is given showing how the company's share price has fared over the last 5 years. The most recent share price, of approximately $2.15 as at 1 March 2019, is considerably lower than its peak as at the start of 2017 when it stood at nearly $7.

3.2 Example tasks

In the real exam each task typically covers more than 1 assessment outcome, and can also cover more than 1 core activity. For simplicity we have taken 1 variant of the May 2019 exam and shown how this might represent core activities and assessment outcomes under the new syllabus.

Please note that not all core activities or associated assessment outcomes are covered; that is not possible due to differences with the old syllabus for strategic case study.

Answers are given at the back of the chapter.

Variant 1 – Task 1

B   Evaluate the business ecosystem and business environment

I can select and apply suitable strategic analytical tools.

and

C   Recommend financing strategies

I can recommend suitable sources of finance.

[Trigger]

Regina Chikaoanda, Denby's Chief Financial Officer, stops by your work space:

[Task]

"Please look at this proposal. Anthony Chan, our Medical Director, is keen to persuade the Board to support this venture. I need you to draft a paper for me that deals with two issues:

First of all, we will have to charge extremely high prices for treatment at the proposed centres in order to cover the cost of providing this level of care. How might we determine whether there would be sufficient demand?

Secondly, we will almost certainly have to borrow the funds needed to set up the Sports Injury Centres. Would it be irresponsible for Denby's Board to borrow the K$130 million required for this purpose?"

[Reference Material]

Proposal to establish sports injury clinics at Denby's Capital City Central and Northern City hospitals

Bardomaz has just launched a new type of ultrasound scanner. A skilled orthopaedic surgeon can use this equipment to assess damaged tissue in cases that would previously have required exploratory surgery to investigate properly. In many cases, a detailed scan will indicate that rest and physiotherapy will be sufficient to cure the injury, but the new scanner can also be used to enable microsurgery, again instead of traditional surgery.

It would cost K$50 million to buy one of these new scanners, to train a surgical team to use it to its full potential and to equip a microsurge by operating suite in the room so that any necessary surgery can be carried out immediately. It is unlikely that the KHS or any of our competitors will make that investment. So far, only two hospitals have acquired it and they are both located in Cornopia.

My proposal is quite ambitious. I propose that Denby should acquire two Bardomaz scanners, one for each of our Capital City Central and Northern City hospitals. Furthermore, we should add specialist physiotherapy suites that are staffed and equipped for managing sports injuries. We would promote these as "Denby Sports Injury Centres". Neither hospital would lose any of its existing facilities.

The new Sports Injury Centres would attract patients from a significant distance. Both cities have many major soccer teams located within a radius of 100 miles. Soccer players frequently suffer from tissue damage arising from wear and tear through training and playing. They also sustain injuries during matches and their employers are always keen to have the best possible treatment. Other professional sportspeople and wealthy amateur sports enthusiasts would be keen to have access to world-leading facilities to treat injuries that might otherwise curtail their playing careers. I believe that the market for these Centres could and would pay a high price for this standard of treatment.

I estimate the total investment, including the cost of the physiotherapy suites, at K$130 million. This is a great deal of money, but Denby has already developed an excellent reputation for the diagnosis and treatment of sporting injuries using more conventional techniques and we should aim to build on that.

Anthony Chan Medical Director

Exercise 1
Write your response to Regina Chikaoanda

Variant 1 – Task 2

A   Develop business strategy

> *I can evaluate strategic options (digital and otherwise)*
>
> *I can recommend response to opportunities and threats arising from digital technologies*

[Trigger]

A month has passed. The proposal to establish the Denby Sports Injury Centres is still being discussed. You receive the following email:

[Task]

From: **Regina Chikaoanda, Chief Financial Officer**

To: **Senior Manager Subject: Sports injuries**

Hi

I have attached a meeting note that I prepared after a discussion with Denby's Head of Orthopaedic Surgery concerning the creation of Denby Sports Injury Centres (DSICs). I need you to draft a briefing paper concerning two issues that follow on from this meeting:

Firstly, should we regard the intellectual property in the form of knowledge and experience developed by our orthopaedic surgeons as a strategic resource that should be protected and preserved?

Secondly, would it be possible to develop an information system that would preserve and share this intellectual knowledge electronically, *even* if Dr Mtimbe's concerns with regard to DSIC prove correct?

Regina

[Reference Material]

Meeting note

Present: Dr Alexander Mtimbe, Head of Orthopaedic Surgery; Anthony Chan, Medical Director; Regina Chikaoanda, Chief Financial Officer

We met at Dr Mtimbe's request, to discuss his concerns arising from the proposal to create two "Denby Sports Injury Centres" (DSICs). Dr Mtimbe pointed out that all of Denby's hospitals have orthopaedic surgery departments, man y of which are regarded as the best facilities in their respective regions for treating sports injuries. All have experience of treating professional sportspeople, including leading soccer players, who often suffer severe injuries.

Dr Mtimbe believes that the doctors, nurses and physiotherapists who presently work in Denby's orthopaedic surgery departments benefit from treating a wide range of patients. Treating highly paid and important sportspeople develops skills that can then be applied to the treatment of other patients. He is concerned that this opportunity will be lost because there will only be two DSICs, which will attract most professional sportspeople away from Denby's other hospitals.

Such technically challenging cases also encourage dialogue between medical staff both within the orthopaedic surgery departments responsible for these patients and between hospitals. Sportspeople always need to make the fullest possible recovery in the shortest possible time and that often forces orthopaedic surgeons to consider slightly unorthodox treatment plans. These provide a strong incentive for senior doctors to consult, both to share experience and also to reduce Denby's liability in the event that the treatment does not work.

Again, that dialogue has created a body of intellectual property that enables Denby to remain at the forefront of orthopaedic surgery. Dr Mtimbe believes that the staff assigned to the DSICs will be too busy with their own patient loads to consult with colleagues from outside the DSICs.

Dr Mtimbe believes that the creation of DSIC will undermine the strength of orthopaedic surgery across Denby.

It was agreed that Dr Mtimbe's concerns would be considered by Denby's Board before any final decision was reached concerning DSIC.

Exercise 2

Write your response to Regina Chikaoanda

Variant 1 – Task 3

B   Evaluate the business ecosystem and business environment

I can recommend responses to economic, political and currency risks

and

C   Recommend financing strategies

I can recommend and apply business valuation models

[Trigger]

A further two months have passed. Denby's Board has agreed to acquire the new scanning equipment and to create two "Denby Sports Injury Centres" (D SICs). You have been asked to attend a special meeting of Denby's Board, in an advisory capacity:

[Task]

John Jenkins, CEO (in the chair)	I have tabled copies of the letter of intent that was couriered to Bardomaz this morning. They insisted on us paying in their home currency. The present exchange rate is C$2.00 = K$1.00, so this will cost us K$100 million.
Regina Chikaoanda, CFO	I am nervous about the potential currency loss on the balancing payment of C$180 million. I think that we need to hedge.
John Jenkins, CEO	I disagree, Regina. Firstly, Cornopia's inflation and interest rates are higher than Keeland's, so the C$ will weaken against the K$, which will make it cheaper to settle the C$180 million balance in nine months. Secondly, I intend to borrow the C$180 million from a Cornopian bank, repayable with fixed interest, over 15 years. That will eliminate any currency risk associated with acquiring and paying for this equipment.
Regina Chikaoanda, CFO *(Turning to you)*	Please evaluate John's arguments with respect to the weakening of the C$ against the K$ exchange rate over the next nine months, and also his argument that arranging a C$180 million fixed rate loan from a Cornopian Bank will eliminate the impact of currency movements.
Robert Borr, Commercial Director *(Turning to you)*	I would also like you to discuss the implications of this project for Denby's share price and whether extending our integrated reporting would help to avoid a fall in share price.

[Reference Material]

DENBY HEALTHCARE

Mr Luis Gonzales

Sales Director

Bardomaz

Millennium City

Cornopia

Dear Luis

Letter of Intent

I am writing to express our intention to place a formal offer for two BardomazExplorer systems. You will install one machine at Denby's Capital City Central Hospital and the other at our Northern City Hospital. You will provide two of our surgical teams with full training in the safe and efficient use of this equipment.

We will pay C$200 million for the equipment and all associated costs of delivery, installation and training. We will make an initial payment of C$20 million when we place a formal order, with the remainder on delivery in nine months' time.

Yours sincerely,

John Jenkins

Chief Executive Officer

Exercise 3

Write your response to Regina Chikaoanda and Robert Borr

Next steps:

(1) You can begin to revisit and revise technical material from your previous studies according to the core activities and assessment outcomes given in this chapter. However we suggest you continue to do this alongside working through the rest of this book so you can also learn how you may need to apply the knowledge.

(2) Remember that you will not be required to perform calculations in the case study exam. However you may need to explain or interpret calculations and so an appreciation of how they are prepared is still relevant and useful. You will also receive credit for any <u>relevant</u> calculations that you choose to produce and interpret in answering a task

(3) In the following chapters we do a complete walkthrough of the prototype sample paper issued in June 2019.

4   Solutions to chapter exercises

Exercise 1

Requirement 1 – demand for sports injury clinics

From Anthony's description, the scanner will offer advantages in terms of speed of recovery from injuries, but will not necessarily cure problems that were previously untreatable. The treatment will have a relatively narrow market in terms of patients who are both willing and able to pay for faster recovery. There is unlikely to be a mass market for this type of treatment. As a starting point, Denby should approach potential buyers, with a view to establishing whether they would be likely to use this service. If their initial response is that they would have little or no need for such an expensive service then Denby should probably regard that as a strong argument not to proceed.

Anthony seems to regard professional soccer clubs as potential clients. The loss of a key player through injury could put a club under significant pressure, both sporting and financial, and so it would be worth establishing whether they would be interested in Denby acquiring this capability. The approach would have to be framed carefully because the clubs are unlikely to make any binding commitment to use this equipment, even if they argue that Denby should acquire it. They could be positive about the principle of Denby making the investment and may then continue to use conventional treatments or fly their players to Cornopia if they require treatment.

Denby needs to conduct a more thorough analysis to determine whether the clubs would have a meaningful incentive to pay for the treatment that could be provided by the new technology, even if that is simply a check on the credibility of any comments made by the clubs.

Denby should start by making contact with major soccer clubs' doctors and physiotherapists in order to discuss the numbers of players who have been injured in recent years. If there are actually very few injuries then that might suggest that there is very little real demand from soccer clubs. If there have been more injuries then the next step is to establish whether the clubs might have used the new technology if it had been available. Denby could ask to discuss case histories of injured players, including prognosis before treatment, the actual outcome and whether the availability of the proposed new technology would have helped. The club could then be asked whether the players were sufficiently valuable to have justified the cost of treatment using ultrasound and microsurgery in order to establish how many referrals each major club might have made on, say, an annual basis.

Denby also has records relating to sports injury patients whom it has treated using conventional means. These records could be studied with a view to determining the number of cases in which the new technology would have had a beneficial clinical effect. Denby could then estimate the net additional cost of using the proposed new equipment compared to the patients' actual billings and also the difference in terms of the outcome of that treatment. Denby could then have identified patients who would have benefitted significantly and could ask them whether they would have paid that additional fee in order to have had that additional expected benefit. It would be ideal if Denby could link the net additional cost to any economic information that the company has about these patients. A professional golfer, say, might be prepared to invest a month's income in securing a more rapid recovery from an injury. It is unlikely that many patients would be willing or able to spend, say, a year's income.

Requirement 2 – borrowing

Borrowing an additional K$130m would increase Denby's gearing from 550/(550 + 1,144) = 32% to (550 + 130)/(550 + 130 + 1,144) = 37%. That is quite a significant increase in gearing, so Denby could find that it is getting close to gearing restrictions in any covenants on existing borrowings. It could also find that the increase causes shareholders some concerns about whether Denby is borrowing too aggressively to fund this project. It probably would be irresponsible for Denby to allow itself to get close to its maximum borrowing capacity or to borrow to the point where the share price starts to fall.

The additional funding will be invested in specialised medical equipment, in modifying physiotherapy suites, and similar costs. Those assets are unlikely to provide the lender with any meaningful security. In the event that Denby becomes unable to service the loan then the assets will undoubtedly have to be sold at a discount. That could mean that Denby is forced to liquidate assets associated to existing, and profitable, areas of the business in the event that the new sports centres fail. The lenders will possibly wish to take security against other assets in any case because they will not be interested in having the right to repossess assets that will have little or no market for resale. Borrowing in this manner will expose other areas of the company to the risks of default and so it may be regarded as a rather reckless thing to do.

Denby's cost of debt, ignoring tax relief, is 22/550 = 4%, so the additional borrowing would increase reduce profit before tax by 130 × 4% = K$5.2 million. That decrease would represent a significant proportion of profit before tax and would be a further argument that the borrowing could be regarded as reckless. The additional finance charge should be considered in the further context of the fixed costs associated with staffing and depreciation of the new equipment. Combining the borrowing costs with the additional expenses will create a significant risk that profits will fall, with an even greater decrease on return on capital employed.

The speculative nature of this project will introduce a speculative element into Denby's revenues and operating profit. That suggests that it would be more prudent to reduce gearing by raising funding from equity. Higher gearing will accentuate any volatility created by the new venture which appears to be a highly volatile proposal. At the very least, Denby should consider its forecast revenues and operating profits and should revisit the gearing decision on the basis of a prudent analysis of the business case.

Examiners comments

Requirement 1 – Demand for sports injury clinics

Candidates should have drawn on the relevant facts that were stated in the scenario, and also trailed to some extent in the pre-seen material. Denby has considerable expertise in treating orthopaedic injuries, but this new venture is intended as a much more ambitious offering that will rely on finding patients who are prepared to pay a considerable premium for a more speedy or more certain recovery.

Marks were awarded for any sensible suggestions as to how demand for this service might be forecast. Stronger candidates might be realistic about some of the difficulties arising from the fact that potential patients/clients have little to lose from claiming that they would use this service and then making alternative arrangements. Answers were not very strong for this requirement. Candidates should have discussed research into possible demand. They could have asked local sports clubs what they thought for example.

They could have sent out surveys or had an interesting website which could have asked about the likelihood of readers using the service. These results could have been examined and used to forecast demand. A number of candidates answered another question which was the reasons why the service would be popular, few marks were awarded for this approach.

Requirement 2 – Borrowing

The question essentially raised two related issues. Borrowing to fund this project will increase gearing. That raises questions about whether the gearing ratio is likely to be increased beyond acceptable limits. Better candidates should have recognised that gearing will increase, but not to the extent that there is a categorical argument that it has become excessive.

The increase in gearing should have been considered against the possibility that the new venture will have an adverse effect on operating profit. It should always be recognised that high gearing is a problem because it intensifies the effect of volatility in operating profit on the profit for the year. If there is no volatility in operating profit then gearing is much less of an issue.

Candidates might also have considered whether lenders would be prepared to accept Denby's assets as security. They may have limited resale value, if a lender could accept the bad publicity associated with foreclosing on a hospital and removing potentially life- saving equipment. This question was done quite well by many candidates with many discussing gearing well. Weaker candidates did

Exercise 2

Requirement 1 – intellectual property

At present, all of Denby's hospitals provide orthopaedic care. This creates a need to attract patients to buy those services. Some patients may be attracted to Denby because they require surgery and do not wish to wait for KHS treatment or are prepared to pay more for the greater comfort and privacy associated with private healthcare. Those patients may not be particularly interested in the expertise of Denby's doctors. They may simply assume that all practising doctors are competent. Straightforward injuries and medical problems that are to be treated by established techniques will probably require little or nothing in the way of consultation between doctors.

Dr Mtimbe's arguments concerning sports injuries do make sense. Sports professionals' careers may depend on making a full and rapid recovery and that may provide an incentive for orthopaedic surgeons to learn and apply the latest developments. The risks of doing so are potentially high, partly because of the ethical risk associated with harming a patient and partly because of the costs and adverse publicity associated with causing further problems. Soccer players and their clubs may be unwilling to take a risk with a proposed treatment unless Denby can claim that it has a successful track record. Developing a list of techniques in which Denby has experienced staff will enable the company to attract more high-profile patients.

There could be a strategic benefit in spreading orthopaedic services across all hospitals. It will, for example, ensure that there is more widespread adoption of the latest techniques into mainstream medicine. Even if patients are not particularly concerned with being treated with the latest techniques, if Denby can help patients recover more quickly and more consistently then it will save costs in the process. Consultation will reduce the potential costs associated with paying damages and adverse publicity because it will be more difficult for a patient to accuse the company of negligence in the event that they do not recover as hoped. Sharing experience will also enable Denby to roll out any new technologies when their costs decrease to the point where they can be used more widely. That could assist Denby to obtain a commercial advantage over the other private hospitals.

It may prove difficult for Denby to safeguard any intellectual property that it creates, thereby reducing its value as a strategic resource. For example, if the DSICs leave Denby with a small number of orthopaedic surgeons who have valuable expertise then Denby's competitors may be tempted to lure them away. Competitors may offer to enhance salaries. They may also be able to offer even more advanced equipment or other desirable benefits that Denby could struggle to compete with. Concentrating advanced skills in the DSICs might also discourage the sharing of knowledge and experience, making the loss of senior doctors even more serious. There will be fewer really senior doctors and so they will be less willing to encourage their colleagues from other hospitals to seek advice. Furthermore, Denby may be unable to prevent its doctors from sharing knowledge with doctors from competing private hospitals.

Medical ethics may forbid doctors from refusing to offer advice when it has been specifically requested.

Requirement 2 – information system

It would be difficult to design a reliable information system that enabled doctors to share their experiences and consult one another in a meaningful way. Dr Mtimbe's point seems to be that doctors often need to consult colleagues because cases differ to a significant extent. For example, the effects of a particular treatment could be affected by the severity of the injury or other aspects of the patient's medical history and so a database that links treatments to situations may not reduce the need for communication between doctors. Such an information system might make it easier to identify colleagues with relevant experience, but it would not necessarily make the relevant information accessible in the manner implied by Regina. Encouraging doctors to seek consultations with colleagues could lead to an inefficient use of time, with constant interruptions. Also, some decisions have to be taken quickly and surgeons are not always available to offer advice when crucial decisions have to be made because, say, they are operating.

The information system will not be as adaptable as direct consultations between experienced doctors. For example, it could be discovered that an accepted treatment carries previously unrecognised risks in certain circumstances. The information system may not make those risks apparent in files relating to cases that had a successful outcome, because the patient could have recovered despite the risks. It is unlikely that the doctors would have followed the advice from the information system blindly in any case, but they will have to consider whether their colleagues were aware of the latest knowledge when they input their cases into the system. Doctors may be reluctant to base decisions on the system if it starts to introduce further complications into reading and interpreting the output.

There could be a significant cost in terms of time and effort to input details into the information system. It will only have value if doctors can establish whether past cases that have been highlighted by the system are relevant to the cases for which they are seeking a consultation. The records will have to be comprehensive to allow for meaningful comparisons between cases on factors such as prior medical history. If doctors resent this inconvenience then they may not give a full account of their cases, potentially undermining the value of the system.

It may be unnecessary to create a separate information system given that Denby will already have detailed medical records online. It may be possible to use Big Data analytics to gather useful insights from existing patient records. One advantage is that the data will be open to re-evaluation in the event that, say, a particular drug is found to have side effects in a particular situation. The system would also reduce the risk that the findings could be biased by anecdotal evidence. For example, a doctor could prescribe a particular drug and believe that it cured the patient when the patient was actually recovering anyway. Big Data analytics would be able to identify whether there was statistical evidence to support the use of a drug in a particular situation. The application of Big Data analytics in these circumstances would, of course, be an information system even if it took a different form from that envisaged by Regina.

Examiners comments

Requirement 1 – Intellectual property

Candidates should probably have considered both sides of this argument, because it is relatively complex.

Denby is in competition with other private hospitals and is also, to an extent, competing for patients' willingness to pay for treatment that would otherwise be provided for free by the KHS. Any form of expertise and skill that the company's doctors can apply to the treatment of patients has the potential to increase revenues.

Better answers should have reflected the fact that medical ethics might make it difficult to withhold information from other hospitals, even if they are in competition with Denby for private patients. Similarly, the doctors themselves are free to leave and it would undoubtedly be impossible to prevent them from drawing on the experience and expertise they developed while working at Denby.

There were some good answers to this requirement. Generally most candidates managed to write something sensible for this requirement.

Requirement 2 – Information system

The pre-seen material highlights some of the complexities of treating patients. Candidates should have recognised that it would be difficult to develop an information gathering system that offered even a fraction of the flexibility associated with a consultation between two or more professional doctors. No two cases are exactly the same and so a database that logs the success or failure of treatment plans will only be of any use if it captures every potentially relevant factor.

Candidates could have seen this as an opportunity to draw upon Big Data Analytics in order to offer an alternative to a traditional information system. It was not, however, mandatory to do so in order to earn full marks.

Very few candidates discussed Big Data in their answers.

Answers to this requirement were surprisingly weak, few candidates seemed to have a good idea what would be involved in developing a good system. Many candidates just achieved a passing score. It was a lack of application and a lack of knowledge which led to lower marks.

Exercise 3

Requirement 1 – exchange rate and foreign currency borrowing

The economic indicators do suggest that the C$ can be expected to weaken against the K$. Purchasing Power Parity Theory suggests that the real cost of goods will be the same regardless of currency. That suggests that a currency that is subject to a high rate of inflation will tend to weaken in order to offset its diminishing purchasing power. Similarly, the International Fisher Effect suggests that the same real rate of interest will be charged on any given currency. Again, that suggests that the C$ will decline against the K$ to compensate for the difference in the interest rates.

John's arguments make sense from a theoretical perspective, but there can be no guarantee that these theories will eliminate the risks. There is empirical evidence to suggest that Purchasing Power Parity Theory and the International Fisher Effect can provide an accurate indication of the direction of any currency change, but they do not offer a precise and accurate forecast of future rates.

Given that the outstanding balance will be C$180m, even a relatively small forecasting error could lead to a significant variation in the amount payable. It is even possible that the Cornopian Government will act to maintain and protect the value of its currency over a relatively short period, such as the nine months that is the case here, and so Denby could suffer a significant additional cost.

Arranging to borrow C$180m will have the effect of hedging the lump sum payment that is due in nine months. Once the loan has been arranged, the lender will settle the amount outstanding as at the due date in full, regardless of any changes in currency values. Given that there is a large balance due and also a potential concern arising from the economic indicators that suggest a currency movement could be forthcoming, it might be prudent to hedge by borrowing in this way. Unfortunately, it will then leave Denby with a commitment to repay the loan with interest over the next 15 years.

Settling the loan will expose Denby to movements between C$ and K$ for an extended period. The interest rate on the loan is fixed, so the C$ payments are known and will be payable over the next 15 years. During that time, there could be significant movements, both strengthening and weakening of the C$. The fact that the lender agreed to a fixed rate loan suggests that the lender anticipates that the C$ will strengthen, which would be associated with a reduction in the C$ interest rate. The only consolation is that the payments extend into the long-term future and so the payments have a low net present value and the additional cost will not start to affect shareholder wealth for some time.

Requirement 2 – share price

The implications for the share price will depend in part on the extent to which the markets believe that this will be a positive NPV investment. In the short term, the announcement of the project will have to be evaluated by the shareholders and they will form an opinion as to whether the investment makes commercial sense. Hopefully, they will be encouraged by the fact that it will give Denby an advantage in competing for the custom of major soccer clubs and professional sports people. Presumably, Denby will make a public announcement of this new service and will describe its advantages, if only to ensure that potential patients are aware of it. That will help the shareholders understand the value of the investment.

This could be regarded as a risky investment, but the shareholders should hold diversified portfolios and so will only be concerned with the systematic risk of the venture. The factors that will affect the success or failure of the DSICs are unlikely to be influenced by factors that affect the stock market as a whole. Their required rate of return may well be lower than that used by the directors in evaluating this project and so the share price may be more likely to increase than decrease. There is, however, always a danger that the shareholders will be concerned that the directors have taken an unacceptable risk or have decided to invest in the project for selfish reasons that could decrease the market value.

Integrated reporting would give the shareholders additional insights into the value creation process. That should make it easier for them to understand the project from the directors' point of view. The shareholders are more likely to share the directors' optimism if the board clarifies the reasoning behind investing in this project. The integrated report should clearly describe the strategic focus and should look more to the future. Such an emphasis will make the board's logic more apparent to the shareholders. A clear explanation of how the centres will fit into Denby's overall strategy will give the shareholders a clearer basis for evaluating and supporting the board's expectations and will, hopefully, enable them to better understand the project's strategic fit.

The integrated report will add to the usual reporting of historical capitals. Giving the shareholders insights into the manufactured capitals will enable them to better understand the new technology and how it will enable the two centres to treat patients more effectively. It will also make it clearer how this technology will assist Denby to compete in this market against other private hospitals. The integrated report will also highlight the impact that the investment will have on intellectual capital, stressing the experience that using this equipment will provide. It will also provide insights into social capital, including the extent to which this project will help Denby develop closer ties to the management of major soccer clubs.

Examiners comments

This section is essentially two pairs of linked requirements. They are presented as two pairs in the question paper, but the answers are shown separately below for the sake of simplifying the marking grid.

Requirement 1 – Exchange rate

The first part of this requirement deals with the PPP theory and the question of whether it might be cheaper to borrow in a foreign currency that might decrease in value.

Candidates should have been able to explain the theory behind this model, as well as indicating some understanding of the empirical evidence concerning its effectiveness in practice. The fact that the model does not work exactly as the mathematics suggest leaves some scope for risk.

There were many very good answers to this question.

Requirement 2 – Foreign currency borrowing

This part effectively asks candidates to consider whether natural hedging might be of value in this scenario. Better candidates will recognise that the timings of the cash flows will disrupt the hedging. This requirement was performed badly with many candidates showing very poor knowledge of this part of the syllabus. Few candidates gave reasonable answers to this requirement. This was mainly due to lack of knowledge.

Requirement 3 – Share price

Candidates may preface their answers with a reference to the Efficient Market Hypothesis (EMH), although that should not have been a major part of this answer.

Better candidates viewed the impact on the share price in terms of the information that is available for the market to process and the extent to which the shareholders agree that this is a sound investment. Weaker candidates were unable to really answer this requirement and offered no more than a surface discussion of EMH. Again, knowledge of this part of the syllabus was surprisingly weak.

Requirement 4 – Integrated reporting

Candidates should know what integrated reporting is, but a detailed description of what it is was not worth many marks unless the description was tied back to the scenario. Few candidates could do much more than briefly mention the six capitals and say integrated reporting was a good idea. Marks were close to the passing score with few high marks being awarded. Candidates knew the theory of integrated reporting but poor at application to the case.

2019 prototype exam – pre-seen information

1   Introduction

The Case Study Examinations are like no other CIMA exam; there is no new syllabus to study or formulae to learn. The best way to be successful at this level is to practise using past case study exams and mock exams based on your real live case study. By reviewing previous case studies alongside your current case you will improve your commercial thought processes and will be more aware of what the examiner expects. By sitting mock exams, under timed conditions you can hone your exam techniques and, in particular, your time management skills.

This textbook is therefore based on this principle. It presents the prototype case study and uses this to demonstrate the skills and techniques that you must master to be successful. The prototype case, Fizz, will be used to walkthrough the processes and approach. The remainder of this chapter contains the Fizz pre-seen material.

We would advise that you skim read this now before moving on to Chapter 4 where you will be provided with more guidance on how to familiarise yourself with the pre-seen material.

Strategic case study exam – 2019 syllabus prototype – pre-seen materials

Contents

You are the Senior Manager in Fizz which is a large company that manufactures soft drinks. Fizz has its head office in Nortland and is quoted on the Nortland Stock Exchange. You report directly to the Board and advise on special projects and strategic matters.

Nortland uses International Financial Reporting Standards.

Nortland's currency is the N$.

The soft drinks market

Any drink that does not contain alcohol is classed as a soft drink.

Retail sales of soft drinks in Nortland amounted to N$12.3 billion in the year to 31 December 2018.

Soft drinks can be split into two main categories: carbonated soft drinks (CSDs) and still drinks. Carbonated soft drinks have carbon dioxide (CO_2) gas dissolved in them in order to create bubbles when they are opened and consumed. Still drinks do not contain CO_2 gas.

CSDs include a wide range of drinks, such as cola, fruit-flavour drinks and sparkling water. Some drinks contain caffeine to make them refreshing. Some contain a high concentration of caffeine or another stimulant and additional sugar so that they can be marketed as "energy drinks". Some CSDs are sold as "mixers" because they are generally mixed with alcohol before consumption.

Still drinks include fruit juice and juice-flavoured drinks, still water, dairy-based drinks such as flavoured milk, and squashes, which are sold as concentrates and are diluted with water before drinking.

Care has to be taken with the words "flavour" and "flavoured" in the food industry. A drink can be sold as, say, "orange flavour" if it tastes like orange juice, even if the flavour has been derived from artificial flavouring. The drink would actually have to contain orange juice in order to be described as "orange flavoured".

Manufacturers have two main distribution channels for their products:

- The off-trade comprises bulk sales to major retailers and wholesalers who supply smaller retailers. The final consumers who buy these drinks will be expected to consume them off the vendor's premises.

  Off-trade products are packaged as cans and bottles, ranging from individual servings of 250ml, 330ml or 500ml up to 1 litre, 2 litre or 3 litre bottles for sharing.

  Some major retailers sell their own-brand drinks alongside branded products from manufacturers such as Fizz. Own-brand products accounted for 23% of the off-trade market by value in 2018.

- The on-trade comprises sales to cafes, restaurants, bars and other outlets where consumers are expected to consume the drinks on the premises. Major on trade outlets will buy directly from the manufacturer, but there are also wholesalers who service the on-trade channel.

- On-trade sales can be in the form of cans or bottles for consumption on the premises or as syrups that are pumped through a soda fountain dispenser that mixes the syrup with carbonated water to create drinks that are sold by the glass. Bars often sell small cans and bottles as mixers, or they can add a small dash of a soft drink from a dispenser.

Retail sales value breakdown

Nortland's overall soft drinks market breaks down by retail sales value as follows:

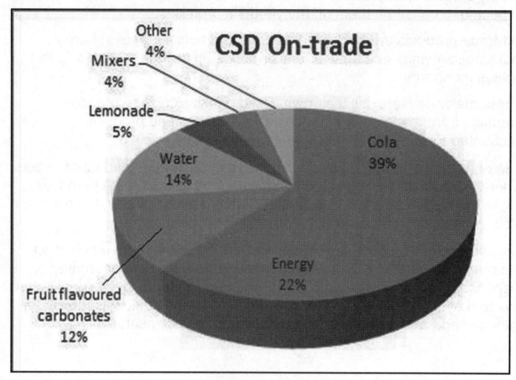

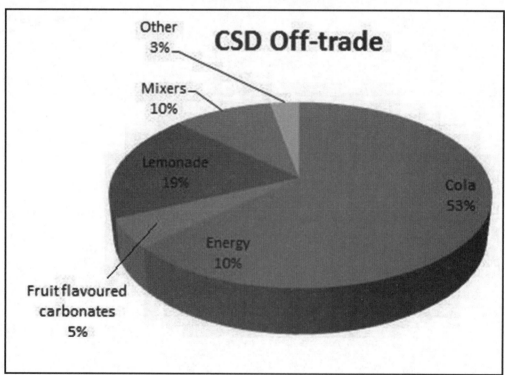

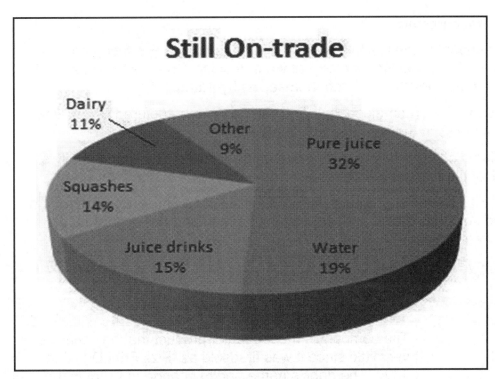

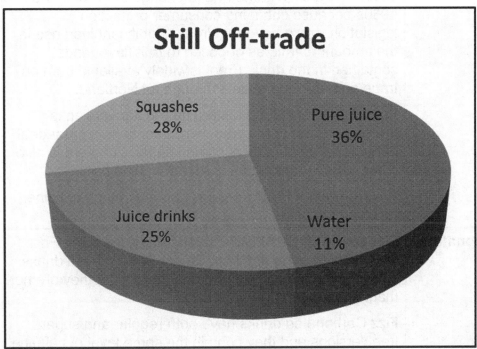

Off-trade sales are split 49% CSD and 51% still by value. On-trade are 72% CSD and 28% still.

Retail sales of soft drinks in Nortland totalled N$12.3 billion in the year to 31 December 2018, of which N$8.2 billion was off-trade and N$4.1 billion was on-trade.

Retail prices are significantly higher for on-trade sales and so on-trade sales account for approximately 10% of soft drink sales by volume, despite being roughly 33% by value

Company background

Fizz was founded by the Clann family in 1890. The company's first products were marketed as refreshing tonics that were designed to settle mild stomach upsets and to help invalids to keep themselves hydrated.

Fizz sells soft drinks (non-alcoholic). The company manufactured 422 million litres of soft drinks in the year to 31 December 2018.

Fizz was listed on the Nortland Stock Exchange in 1962. The Clann family still holds 18% of the company's shares.

Several of Fizz's earliest products are still in production, most notably Froot, a carbonated soft drink that is very popular in Nortland and has a growing global market.

The company's main products are:

CSD (carbonated) drinks	
Froot	The company's most popular product that has changed very little since it was first sold as "Fizz Fruit Drink" in 1890. The drink's name had to change to Froot in the 1960s because changing consumer protection legislation would have required a significant increase in the amount of fruit, as opposed to fruit flavourings, contained in the drink. Froot is widely available from on-trade and off-trade outlets throughout Nortland.
	Froot has a refreshing taste. The regular version is sweetened with corn syrup, which contains a great deal of fructose, a naturally occurring sugar, but there is also a sugar-free version that is sweetened artificially.
	A 330ml can of Froot contains about as much caffeine as a cup of coffee.
Fizz Carbonated	Fizz sells a range of carbonated drinks, including Fizz Cola, Fizz Orange and Fizz Cream Soda. These drinks sell steadily through the off-trade sector, but they are not market leaders.
	Fizz Carbonated drinks have both regular and sugar free versions and they contain the same level of caffeine as Froot.
Funn	Funn is a range of energy drinks that are marketed primarily at consumers in their teens and early 20s. A can of Funn contains a significant quantity of sugar to give the consumer an energy boost and a concentrated shot of caffeine, equivalent to drinking three cups of coffee or three cans of a traditional carbonated drink such as Froot.

Still drinks	
Clann Cordial	Clann Cordial is a concentrated drink that is mixed with water before consumption. It comes in a range of fruit flavours. It is sold through the off-trade channel.
Joocy Juice	Joocy Juice is a range of real fruit juices that are sold in 1 litre cartons.
	Juicy Juice is a premium brand. It is made by harvesting fruit and having it pressed locally. The resulting juice is then packaged into cartons immediately and shipped to Nortland for sale.
	Fizz's competitors use concentrated juice. They extract the juice and then evaporate away most of the water content. The concentrated juice is then shipped to Nortland in tanks. The juice is reconstituted by adding water before packaging it in cartons. This process is far cheaper, but the process affects the flavour of the juice and removes some of its vitamin content. Joocy Juice is made by extracting the juice and packaging it onsite. The resulting juice is said to taste better and have a higher vitamin content because it has not been processed to extract the water.

In addition, Fizz sells Clann Spring Water in both carbonated and still versions. The water is collected from a spring that surfaces in a plot of land close to Fizz's factory in Nortland. Both still and carbonated water is packaged in cans and bottles for sale through off-trade and ontrade.

Fizz is one of the largest manufacturers of soft drinks in Nortland.

Fizz's main competitor is Qwench which manufactures its own range of CSDs and still drinks. Qwench also has the franchise to bottle and sell a global-brand of cola drink. The cola drink's manufacturer makes and sells its drink in the USA. It achieves global sales by selling its drink as a concentrated syrup, which it sells in bulk to a designated franchisee in each national market. The franchisee dilutes the syrup with carbonated water and sells it in bottles and cans that are identical to those made by the original manufacturer. Qwench generates 45% of its revenues from this franchising arrangement.

The manufacturing process

Carbonated drinks, including Froot, are largely water, although this is combined with a host of other ingredients that are necessary to create not only the flavour, but also the colour and the physical sensations associated with consuming these drinks. For example, acids not only preserve the product, they create a sharpness to the drink and stimulate saliva flow.

The water used in the drinks must be very pure. Apart from health risks, any impurities or bacteria could taint the flavour and could result in rapid deterioration, including clouding of the product which would make it unsaleable. Fizz filters and sterilises all water.

There is a cooking process to create the syrup that provides the colour and the distinctive taste of each drink. The syrups are highly concentrated so that they can be combined with the purified water and the sugar or artificial sweeteners to create the basic drink. All that needs to be done to complete the production process is the addition of CO_2.

Finally, the carbonated drinks are bottled or canned and the filled containers are sealed to prevent the escape of the CO_2 gas.

Clann Cordial is made in a very similar manner, although there is a much higher concentration of syrup and the product does not contain CO_2.

All of Fizz's carbonated drinks and cordials are manufactured at a single factory, with several production lines. The factory has canning and bottling facilities on site and a distribution centre.

Joocy Juice is made by pressing fresh fruit, with the resulting juices filtered and packaged immediately by third parties located close to the origin of the juice. The packaged juices are shipped to Nortland. The logistical arrangements for the transportation and delivery of the juices are managed by Fizz's distribution centre. Some of the juice is delivered directly to customers, such as major supermarkets. The remainder is delivered to the distribution centre at Fizz's factory.

Administration and systems

Fizz relies heavily on an integrated suite of enterprise software to manage every aspect of its operations. The software manages all aspects of internal and external communications and all aspects of the administration of Fizz's supply chain.

The information systems monitor inventory levels and schedule purchases and manufacturing accordingly. Routine purchases are managed using Electronic Data Interchange, with orders placed and suppliers' invoices settled electronically. The system also manages sales, checking customer's credit, creating despatch instructions, monitoring customer balances and tracking receipts.

The system captures data and maintains all reporting systems for both internal management reports and external financial reporting. The system can prepare detailed management reports. It can prepare detailed analyses at management's request, without the need for complicated programming. This flexibility enables management to plan ahead.

The Board relies on the information from this system to inform budgeting and forecasting processes and for inputs into the company's enterprise risk management system.

The company's servers are located in a secure building that is adjacent to the factory. All data is backed up to a remote location that is managed by a specialist third-party cloud service provider.

Internal audit

Fizz's internal audit department comprises a team of 14 audit professional staff and four administrative staff. Eleven of the professional staff are qualified accountants and the remainder are trainees who are registered as students.

The Chief Internal Auditor reports to Michelle Adams, who is one of Fizz's non-executive directors and is the convener of the Audit Committee. The Chief Internal Auditor attends all meetings of the Audit Committee in an advisory capacity to speak on any matters arising from the internal audit programme and any internal audit reports. The Chief Internal Auditor does not have a vote.

Cost of making a can of Froot

The costings of making a 330ml can of Froot are as follows:

	N$
Raw materials	
Carbonated water	0.0038
High fructose corn syrup	0.0788
Colouring	0.0074
Phosphoric acid	0.0045
Natural flavours	0.0900
Caffeine	0.0023
Aluminium can	0.0500
Total materials	0.2386
Labour	0.0300
Manufacturing overheads	0.0250
Shipping	0.0600
Total cost	0.3518

Fizz also sells Froot in 500ml cans, 1 litre and 2 litre bottles and as cartons of concentrated syrup for sales to bars, cafes and restaurants that are equipped with soda fountains.

Organisation Chart

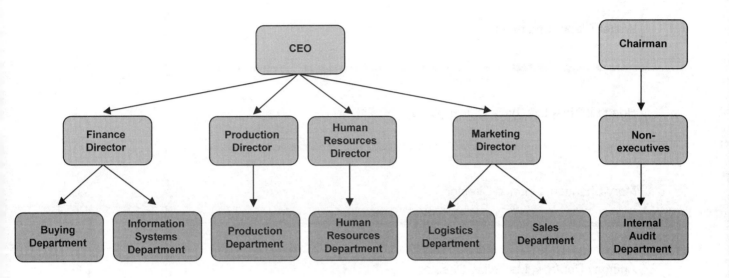

Fizz's board

Walter Clann, Chairman

Hong Li, Chief Executive Officer (CEO)

Mary Shannon, Finance Director

Anthony Renfrew, Marketing Director

Simon Bridges, Production Director

Gayle Forbes, Human Resource Director

Dora Matthews, Non-Executive Director

Bilal Bhatti, Non-Executive Director

Donald Froost, Non-Executive Director

Michelle Adams, Non-Executive Director

Risk register extracts

Risk	Likelihood 1=Unlikely 5=Very likely	Severity 1=Minor impact 5=Major impact	Risk factor (LxS) Low risk 1-8 Medium risk 9-14 High risk 15-25	Control	Responsibility
Operational					
Problems with product safety.	2	4	8	Constant quality checks are conducted at each stage in the manufacturing process.	Production manager
Supplies of raw materials may be interrupted.	3	4	12	Fizz takes pride in selecting only high quality and dependable suppliers.	Chief buyer
Failure of key IT systems.	3	5	15	Fizz maintains backup systems.	IT manager
Disruption of deliveries.	3	5	15	Fizz works closely with all relevant authorities and monitors factors such as the weather.	Logistics manager
Commercial					
Intellectual property rights may be compromised.	3	3	9	Fizz invests in trademark and other forms of protection. Legal enforcement is used when necessary.	Board

Commercial continued					
Legislation or tax penalties to discourage the sale of high calorie products.	2	5	10	Fizz maintains good relations with government.	Board
Changing consumer tastes may lead to declining sales.	4	5	20	Fizz conducts constant market research.	Sales manager
Financial risks, including volatility in currency and commodity prices.	4	5	20	Financial markets are kept under constant review.	Finance manager

Board committees

Audit	The Audit Committee is responsible for Board oversight of the integrity of Fizz's financial reporting process, the Group's system of internal controls,
	Group risk management and the quality of the Group's internal and external audits.
	The Audit Committee reviews the internal audit department's annual work programme, discussing priorities and areas of emphasis with the Chief Internal Auditor. The Audit Committee also receives copies of all internal audit reports and seeks explanations for any significant problems or failures that are reported.
	The Audit Committee oversees Fizz's enterprise risk management (ERM) programme. The Audit Committee periodically receives reports on and discusses governance of Fizz's approach to risk management and the effectiveness of the associated processes.
	The Audit Committee meets the partner responsible for the external audit in order to discuss the planned approach to forthcoming audits and also to discuss the key findings from completed audits.
Compensation	The Compensation Committee takes responsibility for the approach taken to Board compensation. The Committee must approve any and all changes to the rewards paid to executive directors. The Committee also ensures that due process is followed with regard to discretionary payments, such as performance-related bonuses and other benefits that are referred to in directors' contracts.
Nomination	The Nomination Committee is responsible for setting criteria for selecting suitable candidates to fill any vacancies on the Board. The Committee is also responsible for preparing shortlists of suitable candidates whose profiles meet those criteria.
	The Committee meets as and when required when vacancies arise. The Committee also meets once every year to discuss succession planning in the event of any departures from the Board.

Fizz strategy

The Board of Fizz is committed to pursuing the following strategies:

Maintain growth in core markets

Fizz is well established in Nortland, selling a wide range of popular soft drinks.

There could be opportunities that would be worth exploiting. For example, demand for bottled water is increasing and the Clann Spring Water brand is not particularly prominent.

Fizz needs to retain the values associated with its product range, whilst ensuring that new products are developed.

Exploit global opportunities

Fizz is essentially a domestic manufacturer, with considerable strength in its Nortland base. Fizz has had limited success in exporting Froot, with most exports being to supply retailers in holiday destinations that are popular with tourists from Nortland, who wish to buy familiar products. It is extremely difficult to break into mainstream drinks retailing.

Develop consumer trust

Soft drinks have been associated with a number of health scares in recent years and Fizz must take care to develop both products and marketing strategies that can overcome such difficulties.

Extracts from financial statements

Fizz
Consolidated income statement
For the year ended 31 December

	2018	**2017**
	N$m	**N$m**
Revenue	336.2	365.3
Cost of sales	(166.4)	(175.6)
Gross profit	169.8	189.7
Operating expenses	(94.0)	(92.3)
Operating profit	75.8	97.4
Finance costs	(1.1)	(0.4)
Profit before tax	74.7	97.0
Tax on profit	(8.7)	(10.3)
Profit for year	66.0	86.7

Fizz

Consolidated statement of financial position

As at 31 December

	2018 N$m	2017 N$m
Non-current assets		
Intangible assets	141.9	109.2
Property, plant and equipment	116.0	109.8
	257.9	219.0
Current assets		
Inventories	21.4	19.8
Trade receivables	68.0	69.8
Cash and cash equivalents	10.4	7.0
	99.8	96.6
Total assets	357.7	315.6
Equity		
Share capital and share premium	17.6	17.6
Retained earnings	255.2	220.0
	272.8	237.6
Non-current liabilities		
Loans	21.3	10.4
Deferred tax	10.1	9.8
	31.4	20.2
Current liabilities		
Trade payables	45.3	47.8
Current tax	8.2	10.0
	53.5	57.8
	357.7	315.6

Extracts from financial statements of Fizz's closest competitor

Qwench

Consolidated income statement

For the year ended 31 December

	2018	2017
	N$m	**N$m**
Revenue	1,690.1	1,882.2
Cost of sales	(703.5)	(753.4)
Gross profit	986.6	1,128.8
Operating expenses	(654.1)	(680.5)
Operating profit	332.5	448.3
Finance costs	(27.2)	(30.9)
Profit before tax	305.3	417.4
Tax on profit	(42.9)	(36.5)
Profit for year	262.4	380.9

Qwench
Consolidated statement of financial position
As at 31 December

	2018 N$m	2017 N$m
Non-current assets		
Intangible assets	702.7	704.6
Property, plant and equipment	332.1	305.0
	1,034.8	1,009.6
Current assets		
Inventories	118.8	109.5
Trade receivables	379.1	359.8
Derivative financial instruments	67.4	–
Cash and cash equivalents	316.3	184.3
	881.6	653.6
Total assets	1,916.4	1,663.2
Equity		
Share capital and share premium	140.3	140.3
Cash flow hedge reserve	68.3	(4.8)
Retained earnings	774.5	592.8
	983.1	728.3
Non-current liabilities		
Loans	340.0	386.3
Deferred tax	49.3	46.1
	389.3	432.4
Current liabilities		
Trade payables	505.1	463.2
Derivative financial instruments	–	4.6
Current tax	38.9	34.7
	544.0	502.5
	1,916.4	1,663.2

Qwench

Accounting policy extracts

Derivative financial instruments

Derivatives are initially recognised at their fair value whenever derivative contracts are entered into. They are subsequently re-measured at their fair values.

The gain or loss on re-measurement to fair value is recognised immediately in the statement of profit or loss, unless they are accounted for under hedge accounting. Where the instruments qualify for hedge accounting, recognition of any resultant gain or loss depends on the nature of the item being hedged.

Where hedge accounting is applicable, Qwench documents the relationship between hedging instruments and hedged items, as well the risk management objectives and strategy. Qwench also documents the basis on which it believes the hedge to be highly effective in offsetting changes in fair values or cash flows of hedged items.

Cash flow hedges

The effective portion of changes in the fair value of derivatives that are designated and qualify as cash flow hedges are recognised in other comprehensive income.

The gain or loss relating to any ineffective portion is recognised immediately in the statement of profit or loss.

Cumulative amounts recognised in other comprehensive income are recycled through profit or loss in the period when the hedged item affects profit or loss.

Share prices for Fizz and Qwench

Some Industry & Market Ratios

	Soft Drink Industry Median	Stock Market Median
Share Price/Sales Ratio	1.77	1.67
Share Price/Earnings Ratio	26.20	20.59
Share Price/Book Ratio	6.05	1.96

Press clippings

Daily News

Are soft drink manufacturers ignoring obesity risks?

The blog site "Fighting Fat" has been running a hugely successful campaign against the sugar in soft drinks that children love. There are now over 500,000 bloggers on the site.

The soft drinks manufacturers are fighting back with their own publicity claiming that parents need to take some responsibility themselves and prevent their children drinking so many sweet fizzy drinks.

Many schools have banned sugary drinks in their snack shops due to parent and government pressure.

Financial Daily News

12th May 2019

Fizz's profits fall

The publication of Fizz's 2018 results saw share prices fall slightly. This was not unexpected and the share price fell only slightly.

The company's Board released a statement reassuring shareholders that trading conditions in 2018 had been difficult due to increasing competition from soft drinks manufacturers overseas and that Fizz had in fact "done well".

Industry analysts noted that Qwench, Fizz's largest competitor, had already reported a far more severe decline in profits and so

Fizz's performance dip had been expected.

Daily News

The True Cost of Sugary Drinks

The increasing incidence of obesity is having a profound effect on the nation's health and is diverting increasing amounts of resources from the health service.

Fatty foods used to be the main cause of obesity, but foods and drinks with high sugar content are emerging as more significant causes.

Governments are increasingly concerned about the rising costs of illnesses such as type 2 diabetes and cancer, which have risen alongside an obesity epidemic. The battle between food companies and governments may be only just beginning; if health systems fail under the strain of obesity-related diseases, regulators will act to prevent rather than treat them afterwards.

Several countries are introducing legislation to help curb intake of sugary foods; health warnings, sales taxes, banning of junk foods in schools, restrictions on advertising to children and reduced portion sizes will become more prevalent.

Daily News

Health Watchdog Issues Warning on Energy Drinks

The current fashion for young adults to drink energy drinks has led to a warning from the medical profession concerning the safety of those drinks.

Energy drinks are sold as "dietary supplements", which means that there are fewer restrictions on the concentration of the stimulants that give them their refreshing properties. Legally, soft drinks cannot contain more than 71mg of caffeine in a can, but there is no legal limit on the quantity that can be added to an energy drink. Some products contain as much as 400mg per can, equivalent to drinking several cups of strong coffee.

Most consumers are aware of the effects of caffeine but many do not realise that energy drinks usually contain other stimulants as well, such as guarana, which is essentially a compound of caffeine. Doctors are concerned that consumers do not fully understand the risks that they are taking.

Dr Surya Prakash, a consultant physician specialising in eating disorders, warned consumers that consuming that quantity of caffeine could increase blood pressure and might affect behaviour. He recommended that consumers should not drink these products on a daily basis and that they should never drink more than one can in a single day.

2019 prototype exam – analysing the pre-seen

Chapter learning objectives

- to understand various techniques and models that can help familiarisation with the pre-seen.

1 The importance of familiarisation

The pre-seen material is released approximately seven weeks before you sit the exam and one of your first tasks will be to analyse the context within which the case is set. Although your responses in the exam will be driven by the unseen material, you will only be able to fully assess the impact of each event on the organisation if you have a sufficient depth of knowledge and awareness of both the organisation and the industry in which it operates.

The purpose of the pre-seen material is to allow you to gain that knowledge and awareness. Remember, you will be acting in the position of a senior finance manager who advises the highest level of management. It will therefore be expected that you will have the same level of familiarisation as someone fulfilling that role.

It is extremely important that you study the pre-seen material thoroughly before you go into the examination. There are two main reasons for this:

- It will save time in the examination itself if you are already familiar with the pre-seen material (there will be approximately 25-30 pages of information in the pre-seen, so a lot of information to absorb).

- It enables you to develop a view of the situation facing the organisation in the case study.

You will not be able to respond to the examination tasks from the pre-seen material alone; the unseen material given to you in the examination will present significant new information that may alter the situation substantially. Even so, a major step towards success in the examination is a careful study, exploration and understanding of the pre-seen material.

Each set of pre-seen material is different but as a general rule, you can expect the following:

- Industry background

- History of the business

- Key personnel

- Organisational structure

- Key risks facing the business

- Financial Statements

- Press articles addressing issues facing the industry

Each of these areas will need reviewing in detail.

You should question what each piece of information tells you, and why the examiner may have given it to you.

2 Exhibit by exhibit analysis

The purpose of this initial stage is to lay a foundation for further analysis. It's more about asking questions than finding solutions. Before you do anything else, you should read the pre-seen material from beginning to end without making any notes, simply to familiarise yourself with the scenario.

Read the material again, as many times as you think necessary, without making notes. You can do this over a period of several days, if you wish.

When you think you are reasonably familiar with the situation described by the material, you should start to make notes. By making notes, you will become more familiar with the detail of the scenario.

- Try to make notes on each paragraph (or each group of short paragraphs) in the pre-seen material.

- Ask yourself "why might the examiner have told me this?"

- Try to make your questions as broad as possible; consider as many different stakeholders as possible and try to put yourself in different positions (say the CEO, a customer, an employee, etc.) to consider the information from different perspectives.

 Illustration 1 – Fizz: Introductory overview

Given below is an example of some questions you could ask yourself relating to the second exhibit of the question tutorial exam pre-seen information.

Question	Potential response
What does Fizz do?	It is a manufacturer of soft drinks (p2)
Is Fizz a well-established company?	It was founded in 1890 and was listed on the Nortland Stock Exchange in 1962 (p6).
Which particular sector of the soft drinks market does it operate in?	Carbonated drinks (Froot, Fizz Carbonated, Funn) and still drinks (Clann Cordial, and Joocy Juice). It also sells spring water in both carbonated and still forms (p.6&7).
How important is IT to Fizz?	Critical – the company relies heavily on an integrated suite of enterprise software to manage every aspect of its operations (p.9)
What are the most significant risks facing the company?	(1) Changing consumer tastes may lead to declining sales; and (2) Financial risks, including volatility in currency and commodity prices. Both of the above have the highest risk factor according to the company's risk register (p.14&15)

3   Note taking

When you're making notes, try to be as creative as possible. Psychologists tell us that using conventional linear notes on their own use only a small part of our mental capacity. They are hard to remember and prevent us from drawing connections between topics. This is because they seek to classify things under hierarchical headings.

Here are some techniques that candidates find useful. See which ones work for you as you practise on the question tutorial case in this text.

Spider diagrams

Spider diagrams (or clustering diagrams) are a quick graphic way of summarising connections between subjects. You cannot put much detail into a spider diagram, just a few key words. However, it does help you to 'visualise' the information in the case material. You must expect to update your spider diagram as you go along and to redraft it when it starts to get too messy. It is all part of the learning process.

Timelines

Timelines are valuable to make sense of the sequence of events in the pre-seen and to understand where the company in the case study presently stands. The case study exam takes place in real time, so you need to be clear how long is likely to elapse between the data in the pre-seen and the actual exam. This is the time period during which the issues facing the company can be incorporated into the unseen material.

Colours

Colours help you remember things you may want to draw upon in the exam room. You could write down all your financial calculations and observations in green whilst having red for organisational and blue for strategic. Some candidates use different colour highlighter pens to emphasise different aspects of the pre-seen material perhaps using the same colour coding suggestion.

Additionally, sometimes making notes in different colours helps you to remember key facts and some of the preparation that you have done using the pre-seen material.

Use whatever colours work for you – but it does help to make notes on both the pre-seen material and the research you do. DO NOT just read the material – you must take notes (in whatever format) and if colours help you to understand and link your research together then use colours.

4 Technical analysis

Now you're reasonably familiar with the material it's time to carry out some technical analysis to help you identify and understand the issues facing the company.

A good starting point is to revise any 'technical' topics that might be relevant. The pre-seen material might imply that a particular 'technical' issue could be relevant in the exam, such as commenting on the corporate governance of a company, financing, hedging, business valuations, and so on. Anticipate exam tasks by asking yourself how you would apply your knowledge in such areas in the context of the live case.

If you lack confidence on any topic that might be relevant, go back to your previous study materials and revise it if necessary.

Exercise 1 – Fizz: technical topic analysis

Typical technical topic areas could include the following.

1 Discuss the financing structure at Fizz (F3).

2 Discuss the level of dividend payout at Fizz (F3).

3 Evaluate the corporate governance structure at Fizz (P3).

4 Discuss Fizz's exposure to currency risk (P3).

5 Identify possible strategies for growth for Fizz (E3).

5 Financial analysis

You will almost certainly be given some figures in the pre-seen material. These might relate to the company's profits or losses, or product profitability. There might be statements of profit or loss and statements of financial position for previous years, statements of changes in equity, cash flow statements, share price graphs, and so on. You might also be given similar information for a competitor.

A key part of your initial analysis will be to perform some simple financial analysis, such as financial ratio calculations or a cash flow analysis. These might give you a picture of changes in profitability, liquidity, working capital management or cash flows over time, and will help ensure you have a rounded picture of the organisation's current position.

If a cash flow statement is not provided, it may be worth preparing a summary of cash flows. You may have to make some assumptions if the detailed information isn't provided but even with these, there is great value in appreciating where the money has come from, and where it is being spent.

Profitability ratios

You might find useful information from an analysis of profit/sales ratios, for:

- the company as a whole

- each division, or

- each product or service.

Profit margins can be measured as a net profit percentage and as a gross profit percentage. ROCE is also a fundamental profitability ratio to be considered. You can then look at trends in the ratios over time, or consider whether the margins are good or disappointing.

Analysing the ratio of certain expenses to sales might also be useful, such as the ratio of administration costs to sales, sales and marketing costs to sales or R&D costs to sales. Have there been any noticeable changes in these ratios over time and, if so, is it clear why the changes have happened?

Working capital ratios

Working capital ratios can be calculated to assess the efficiency of working capital management (= management of inventory, trade receivables and trade payables). They can also be useful for assessing liquidity, because excessive investment in working capital ties up cash and slows the receipt of cash.

The main working capital ratios are:

- "inventory days" or the average inventory holding period: a long period might indicate poor inventory management

- "receivable days" or the average time that customers take to pay: a long period could indicate issues with the collection of cash, although would need to consider this in light of the entity's credit terms and industry averages

- "payable days" or the average time to pay suppliers: a long period could indicate cash flow difficulties for the entity, although would need to consider in light of credit terms.

You should be familiar with these ratios and how to calculate the length of the cash cycle or operating cycle.

Cash flow analysis or funding analysis

If the main objective of a company is to maximise the wealth of its shareholders, the most important financial issues will be profitability and returns to shareholders. However, other significant issues in financial strategy are often:

- cash flows and liquidity, and

- gearing

A possible cash flow problem occurs whenever the cash flows from operations do not appear to be sufficient to cover all the non-operational cash payments that the company has to make, such as spending on capital expenditure items.

An analysis of future funding can be carried out by looking at the history of changes in the statement of financial position.

Ratio analysis – a warning!

Candidates are advised to resist typing out ratios in the exam unless they are actually relevant to the task. It's always impressive when a candidate uses a ratio to reinforce a point, but it's a waste of time to produce a couple of ratios just because you can!

Exercise 2 – Fizz: Ratio Analysis

Use ratio analysis to assess the profit performance of Fizz for 2017 and 2018, and compare it to that of Qwench. Write a brief commentary on your findings.

6 Industry analysis and research

Why is industry research important?

Remember, part of your preparatory work is to analyse the context within which the case is set. A full analysis is not possible without an understanding of the industry and research may support the information provided in the pre-seen. From this analysis, you may be better able to understand the key issues and address the requirements.

The pre-seen material usually contains a good summary of relevant information about the industry. This can be relied on as accurate at the time it is published and will form the basis of your analysis. At the strategic level the scope of this industry information will be fairly extensive, as the industry data provided with the pre-seen will be more detailed and varied to support analysis of the business from a strategic perspective.

You could further research the industry setting for the case you are working on so that you can develop a better understanding of the problems (and opportunities) facing companies in this industry. Hopefully, it will also stop you from making unrealistic comments in your answer on the day of the exam.

Industry research will allow you to add further comments in terms of:

- identifying potential problems currently facing the industry

- identifying the nature of competition and the basis for customer and supplier relationships

- considering the competitive strategies being followed by companies operating in the real world and how they are achieved (e.g. special technologies, use of brands) and whether they could be adopted by the company in the pre-seen

- identifying issues with operational aspects of real world firms.

How to conduct industry research

Your research could incorporate any of the following sources of information:

- *Personal networks / experience*

  If you happen to work in the industry described, then you could talk to colleagues about the case. If not, then perhaps family or friends with relevant experience could help.

  Alternatively, it may be that you have been a customer in the industry described. For the sample paper, many students would have had experience of being a gym member and so would appreciate some of the issues involved.

- *Using the Internet*

  This is the most convenient and commonly used method of researching the industry, but as noted above, try to target the information you're looking for in order to avoid wasting time. Generally, you will be looking for the following sorts of information:

  - Websites of firms similar to the one(s) in the pre-seen material. This can help you learn about the sorts of products and competitive strategies they follow and may also yield financial information that can be compared with the data in the pre-seen material.

  - Trade journals of the industry in the pre-seen. This will provide information on real world environmental issues facing the business.

  - Articles on the industry in journals and newspapers. These will keep you up to date on developments.

  - Financial statements of real firms, perhaps even calculating key ratios.

Illustration 2 – Fizz: Real world websites

Relevant websites for the soft drinks industry include the following:

The Industry

http://www.britishsoftdrinks.com/

http://www.britishsoftdrinks.com/write/mediauploads/publications/bsda_annual_report_2015.pdf

http://www.foodbev.com/news/is-2016-the-year-that-the-soft-drinks-market-grows-up/

https://www.ft.com/content/8521da6e-ec5a-11e5-bb79-2303682345c8

http://www.bbc.co.uk/news/magazine-35831125

http://fortune.com/2016/03/29/soda-sales-drop-11th-year/

http://www.pci-mag.com/features/featuretrends-in-the-carbonated-soft-drinks-market-4775235

http://www.foodmanufacture.co.uk/Ingredients/Drinks-manufacturers-target-sophisticated-adult-soft-drinks-market

http://www.newfoodmagazine.com/25233/news/industry-news/lovely-drinks-all-natural-colas/

http://www.bbc.co.uk/news/uk-33783942

http://www.telegraph.co.uk/news/2016/09/19/on-the-go-milk-bottles-to-compete-with-bottled-water-and-fizzy-d/

http://www.telegraph.co.uk/business/2016/04/16/tight-squeeze-in-smoothie-land-despite-falls-in-sugar-consumptio/

http://www.telegraph.co.uk/food-and-drink/features/cold-pressed-charcoal-new-health-juice-drinking-2017/

Soft Drink Companies

http://www.telegraph.co.uk/finance/newsbysector/retailandconsumer/12124206/Britvic-sales-lose-their-fizz-after-tough-trading-in-Europe.html

http://www.bbc.co.uk/news/business-36096148

https://www.pepsico.com/docs/album/annual-reports/pepsico-2015-annual-report_final_s57dqszgmy22ggn.pdf?sfvrsn=0

http://news.bbc.co.uk/1/hi/uk/3523303.stm

http://www.telegraph.co.uk/business/2016/10/16/highland-spring-sales-fizz-as-thirst-for-bottled-water-overtakes/

http://www.telegraph.co.uk/finance/businessclub/12021474/Welsh-drinks-company-to-double-capacity-to-meet-demand-for-water.html

http://www.radnorhills.co.uk/home

http://www.telegraph.co.uk/football/2016/12/26/west-ham-turned-650m-takeover-bid-red-bull/

http://www.agbarr.co.uk/

Health

http://www.telegraph.co.uk/food-and-drink/healthy-eating/11-reasons-to-stop-drinking-fizzy-drinks/

http://www.weight-masters.com/say-no-to-fizzy-drinks.html

http://www.bbc.co.uk/news/health-35880639

http://www.bbc.co.uk/news/uk-wales-south-east-wales-36638596

http://www.telegraph.co.uk/news/2016/06/01/red-bull-addict-who-drank-20-cans-a-day-has-liver-so-damaged-doc/

7 Ethical analysis

Ethical issues could relate to any of the following areas:

- corporate social responsibility;
- personal ethical behaviour of individuals in the case;
- business ethics.

Before the exam, you should take some time to remind yourself of CIMA's Guidelines on ethical conduct. You can download a copy of the Ethical Guidelines from CIMA's website, if you want to read the full text. Although these are useful, you must remember that the ethical issues in the exam are not necessarily ethical issues facing the management accountant, but more issues facing the business as a whole. An awareness of general 'corporate ethics' and 'corporate and social responsibility' will therefore be beneficial.

Illustration 3 – Fizz: Real world ethical issues

Online research into the soft drinks industry quickly reveals ethical (and legal) issues related to sugar content in soft drinks. For example:

https://www.theguardian.com/lifeandstyle/2016/nov/15/half-of-fizzy-drinks-have-more-sugar-in-one-can-than-adult-daily-limit

8 Position audit

Once you've analysed all of the above you're ready to carry out a position audit.

CIMA defines a position audit as:

Part of the planning process which examines the current state of the entity in respect of:

- resources of tangible and intangible assets and finance,
- products brands and markets,
- operating systems such as production and distribution,
- internal organisation,
- current results,
- returns to shareholders.

What you should be attempting to do is stand back so you can appreciate the bigger picture of the organisation. You can do this by considering four main headings – Strengths, Weaknesses, Opportunities and Threats. This is usually referred to as a SWOT analysis. Within your SWOT analysis you should look for:

- Threat homing in upon weakness – the potential for failure.

- Threat on a strength – should be able to defend against it but remember competencies slip.

- Opportunity on a strength – areas they should be able to exploit.

- Opportunity on a weakness – areas where they could exploit in the future if they can change.

In addition to preparing a SWOT analysis, it is useful to prepare a two-three page summary of your analysis. Try not to simply repeat information from the pre-seen but add value by including your thoughts on the analysis you've performed.

Exercise 3 – Fizz: SWOT analysis
Perform a SWOT analysis for Fizz.

9 Main issues and précis

Once you've prepared your summary you are finally able to consider the key issues facing the organisation. Your conclusion on the main issues arising from the pre-seen will direct your focus and aid your understanding of issues in the exam.

Once you've got a list of the main issues, give yourself more time to think. Spend some time thinking about the case study, as much as you can. You don't have to be sitting at a desk or table to do this. You can think about the case study when you travel to work or in any spare time that you have for thinking.

- When new ideas come to you, jot them down.

- If you think of a new approach to financial analysis, carry out any calculations you think might be useful.

Remember, all of the above preparatory work enables you to feel as if you really are a management accountant working for this organisation. Without the prep, you're unlikely to be convincing in this role.

Illustration 4 – Fizz: Summary

Fizz was founded in 1890 by the Clann family, who still own 18% of the issued share capital. It floated on the Nortland Stock Exchange in 1960. It is therefore a well-established company, and has developed a stock market reputation over almost 60 years.

The industry

Information is given about the soft drinks market, and how it can be categorised. Firstly, the drinks themselves can be categorised in two ways: carbonated soft drinks (CSDs), and still drinks. Secondly, manufacturers such as Fizz have 2 main distribution channels: off-trade, which is selling to retailers and wholesalers; and on-trade, which is selling to cafes, restaurants, bars and the like.

Detailed information is given about how the market is broken down in Nortland for both of these 2 categories of soft drink sales (notice that this analysis is for the country, not for Fizz).

The total market sales of soft drinks in Nortland in 2018 was N$12.3 billion, of which 2/3 was off-trade and 1/3 on-trade.

The company

Fizz is described as one of the largest soft drinks manufacturers in Nortland, making 422 million litres of soft drinks in the year to 31 December 2018.

Fizz has a diversified product portfolio, making both CSDs and still drinks. Its main CSDs are: Froot, which has been around since the company began and comes in both traditional and sugar-free variants; Fizz Carbonated, which covers a range of flavours and also comes in traditional and sugar-free formats; and Funn, a high energy drink aimed at teenagers and those in their early 20s. All 3 of these brands contain significant levels of caffeine.

The main still drinks are: Clann Cordial, which comes in a range of fruit flavours and sold through the off-trade channel; and Joocy Juice, which is a premium brand fruit juice.

In addition, mention is made of Clann Spring Water, which is sold in both still and carbonated versions. This comes from a spring close to Fizz premises.

Information is given about the manufacturing process; not surprisingly, quality control is paramount. Fizz has 1 factory for its CSDs and cordials, and a number of production lines within. It also has canning and bottling facilities on site, and a distribution centre.

Costings are provided for making 1 can of Froot; attention should be given for signs of increasing costs e.g. corn syrup (a commodity), or the introduction of additional taxes.

Fizz has a functional structure, and a breakdown of the Board is provided. There are a number of non-executive directors, although there is not quite an equal balance between EDs and NEDs.

The company maintains a risk register, identifying the main risks to the business and assessing them on the basis of likelihood and impact. Responsibilities for each risk are assigned, together with ways in which to mitigate. The key risks identified are changing consumer tastes and financial risks (such as volatility in the price of commodities or currencies).

The Board has committed to pursuing 3 main strategies: maintaining growth in core markets (with spring water identified in particular); international growth; and developing consumer trust through the quality and safety of its products.

The competitor

Qwench is Fizz's main competitor, and seems to operate in the same product areas as Fizz. However, it also has a franchise for a global cola brand, from which it derives 45% of its revenues. The accounts for both companies are provided, enabling a comparison in size and performance to be made. Qwench is a much bigger business; its revenue for 2018 is over 5 times that of Fizz.

Information is given on how the shares of Fizz and Qwench have performed over the 12 months to 30 April 2019. Fizz' share price is largely unchanged, but that of Qwench has fallen by around 20%.

Information is given on share price data for both the soft drinks industry and the stock market as a whole. Soft drinks as a sector has a higher than average value. This information would prove useful were a valuation exercise need to be carried out.

Finally, there are a number of newspaper articles shedding further light on the industry. Not surprisingly, much of this focuses on the health aspects of certain drinks, and mention is made of the ways in which some governments are looking to combat this issue.

10 Summary

You should now understand what you need to do in order to familiarise yourself with the pre-seen sufficiently.

Test your understanding answers

Exercise 1 – Fizz: technical topic analysis

1   Discuss the financial gearing structure at Fizz.

The gearing level refers to how much of the company's funds come from borrowings (debt) rather than from the shareholders (equity). It is best measured as the ratio of debt: debt + equity, and should be based on market values rather than book values.

The relative costs

Using debt funds is cheaper than equity for two reasons.

Firstly, the debt investors require a lower rate of return on their investment as the risk involved in the investment is lower than the risk involved in equity investment. The debt investors know they will receive the same amount of interest each year regardless of the company's performance; whereas the return the equity investor gets varies with the company's fortunes.

Secondly, the interest the company pays on its debt is a tax allowable expense (dividends are not).

This effectively means that the tax authorities are paying part of the expense thus reducing the final, after tax, cost even further.

The effect on equity

The above would seem to suggest that a company should use as much debt as possible (rather than equity) to fund its operations. Doing so would apparently reduce the average cost of funding the operations as we'd be using a high proportion of cheaper funds. (This average cost is called the Weighted Average Cost of Capital – WACC.)

Unfortunately it's not that simple. Increasing the proportion of debt funds will cause the rate of return required by the shareholders (the cost of equity) to rise. This is because the need to pay higher (and constant) amounts of interest increases the volatility of the equity returns. That is, it increases the risk of the equity investors (called financial risk), which in turn increases the rate of return they want.

The end result

Thus increasing the proportion of debt funds will have two opposing effect on WACC. The increased proportion of cheaper debt funds will tend to reduce WACC, but at the same time the resulting increased cost of the equity funds will tend to increase it. The end result (whether WACC increases or decreases) therefore depends on the relative size of these two opposing effects.

The importance of this is that a lower cost of capital (WACC) means the company's earnings will be discounted by the market at a lower rate thus increasing the total market value of the company. That increase will be reflected in a higher share price.

Despite theoretical arguments to the contrary, it is generally accepted that at low levels of debt an increase in debt funding will reduce WACC but at high levels any further increase in debt funding will increase WACC. There is no theoretical way to find the optimum level.

The gearing effect

The presence of debt finance "gears up" the effect of changes in earnings on the shareholders. A given increase in company earnings will result in a bigger increase in equity earnings. Thus if company earnings are increasing this is desirable, but the reverse is also true. If earnings fall a high level of gearing will result in a larger fall in equity earnings which is of course disadvantageous to the shareholders.

This effect can be seen by comparing Fizz's most recent results with those of Qwench. Whilst both companies have seen an almost identical fall in Return on Capital Employed (ROCE), Qwench has seen a much larger decline in Return on Equity.(Qwench's Return on equity has almost halved whereas ours has dropped by just one third.) This difference is likely to be due, at least in part, to the much higher level of gearing in Qwench.

The practicality

There are a number of practical considerations involved in the decision on the gearing level but the main one is the company's "debt capacity". This essentially means how much debt the market is prepared to give the company. This will itself depend on a number of factors (such as credit ratings, available security, and interest cover), but a reasonable guide to the best level of gearing is to look at what other companies in the same industry are doing.

This is likely to be what Fizz's key investors are doing.

Conclusion

Compared to Qwench, Fizz's current level of gearing is indeed very low. However, Qwench has reduced its gearing level over the last twelve months which may indicate that they are at the top end of acceptable levels for the industry rather than typical. Nonetheless Fizz's current level of gearing (at just 7.24% by book value) would likely be seen as low by any standard.

Whilst this has protected Fizz shareholders from the recent fall in performance, it may not be appropriate for the future. It is possible that the Fizz institutional investors (who may be seen as the "professionals") might be pushing for increases would support this view, and the fact that the Fizz share price has largely remained stable despite the recent poor results indicates that the market has confidence in the company's future performance and growth.

Considering the matter from the debt investors' perspective, it would appear that Fizz would have no difficulty raising further debt. It has tangible assets to offer as security well in excess of its current debt level (unlike Qwench) and interest cover is currently very high.

On balance it would seem that an increase in Fizz's gearing level would be beneficial.

2 Discuss the level of dividend payout at Fizz.

Introduction

Reduced to basics, the dividend decision is a balancing act. Given a certain amount of available profit, the question is how much should be paid to the shareholders and how much is needed to finance the future growth of the company? On the face of it, more dividends means less available for future investment and therefore lower levels of future growth (and therefore less profit available to pay future dividends).

However, this is further complicated by the availability of other sources of funds. If, for example, debt funds could be used to finance the future growth then less of the profit is needed so more can be paid as dividend.

The theory

There is no real theoretical answer to this balancing problem. The available theory (Modigliani & Miller's dividend irrelevance theory) claims that it's not a problem; if the company has available investment opportunities with positive NPVs then these should take precedence over dividends. However, the theory depends on a number of assumptions (the key ones being no differential taxes and no transaction cost) which are simply not valid in practice.

Thus the theory is of little practical use.

Possible choices

There are a number of different policies that could be followed. The main choice is between:

*   Residual dividend:

    Here any available profits are first used to invest in positive NPV projects. A dividend is only paid if there are profits left after all available positive NPV projects have been undertaken.

    (This is following the theory mentioned above.)

*   Constant pay-out ratio:

    Each year the dividend paid is a fixed proportion of that year's available profit.

*   Stable dividends:

    The company pays a constant dividend each year, or a dividend growing at a constant rate.

The first two of these end up with varying and largely unpredictable dividends and if there is one thing the markets hate it is uncertainty (or risk). A stable dividend policy enables investors to predict with reasonable certainty what the return will be each year.

The practicality

In reality there are two main considerations:

- The clientele effect:

  This is the idea that, over time, a company with a given dividend policy (whatever that may be) will attract as its shareholders those investors who want that particular policy. Thus whatever policy the company chooses it should stick to it.

- The signalling effect:

  The shareholders think that the dividend declared each year reflects the directors' confidence in the future performance of the company. Thus dividends should not be varied year on year just because of short term fluctuations in company performance.

Both these considerations again reflect what was said above; stability is what investors want.

Fizz's situation

With a steady growth rate in dividends Fizz is giving investors the stability that they want, and the company should be very careful of any change in its policy. It is also in fact following the same policy that the majority of quoted companies follow which suggests its approach is the right one.

Fizz's latest dividend proposal represents a pay-out ratio of 47% (compared to Qwench at 20%) and provides a dividend yield of 2.85% (compared to Qwench at <2%). With the higher figures Fizz shareholders are likely to be much happier and its cash balance at N$10.4m would not be considered excessive. Additionally, unlike Qwench, the Fizz share price has hardly changed over the last twelve months which would indicate that its shareholders are happy with the status quo.

Conclusion

As stated above, the dividend decision involves striking a balance between paying dividends and retaining profit to finance expansion. The evidence would suggest that Fizz has that balance about right.

3 Evaluate the corporate governance structure at Fizz (P3).

Board Balance

A Board should be balanced in terms of skills, experience and diversity. Such a structure helps enable Fizz's Board to deal with strategic and operational issues.

Little is known of the background regarding the Non-Executive Directors (NEDs) nor the Executives. Though we are told of the roles executives perform at Fizz, we do not know their experience. As a result, an evaluation of the balance in terms of Board skills cannot be made.

A Board should also be balanced in terms of the number of Executive and NED roles. There should be the same number of NEDs as Executives (excluding the Chair), that is, Executive Directors should not outnumber the NEDs. In order to ensure the NEDs represent the interests of the shareholders, they should be independent.

Fizz only has 4 NEDs versus 5 Executive (excluding the Chair) therefore this criteria is not met. In addition, there is no information regarding the independence of the NEDs. (See also the role of the Chairman later). NEDs are meant to challenge the Executives and act on behalf of the shareholders. This is less likely to happen at Fizz if firstly, there are not enough NEDs and secondly, they are possibly not independent.

Good corporate governance should ensure that a company is run in the interests of the shareholders. The Clann family still owns 18% of the company's shares which is a significant proportion. The Chairman, Walter Clann, may be one of these family shareholders. There are pros and cons to this arrangement. It could be argued that Mr Clann can represent the group of people that are (probably) majority shareholders well as he is likely to be in close contact with them. In this way, it is unlikely he would allow for anything detrimental to happen to the company and the shareholders needs are met. However, he is not the only shareholder. The remaining shareholders (82%) may disagree with the way the company is being run and they have a limited means of making their voice heard as the Chairman is not independent and the NEDs may also not be independent.

CEO and Chairman roles

These roles have been split at Fizz which is compliant with most countries' Corporate Governance guidance.

The Chairman's role is to run the Board, the CEO's role is to run the company. Placing both positions in one person's hands may give them too much power. Given that there are not enough Non-Executive Directors (NEDs) to keep such power "in check", it is important that it is not held in one person's hands.

The Chairman is a founding family member and though this has benefits in terms of truly having the company interests at heart, it does not necessarily mean he has the ability to perform the role. The Chairman should run the Board meaning he is expected to set an agenda for the Board such that is it forward-looking in terms of its strategy as well as ensuring the current business is well evaluated and overseen. In many companies, the Chairman would be expected to manage Board meetings so that they are an efficient and effective use of Director time. Management and organisation skills are essential but may not be present in Walter Clann by virtue of his being a member of the founding family.

The Chairman would also be expected to be the representative for the shareholders - they should be able to communicate to the Chairman on matters of concern. However, when the Chairman is not independent, as is the case at Fizz, the Board should appoint a Senior Independent NED to perform this role. There is no evidence in the case that one of the existing NEDs performs this role.

Committees

We are given information about three Board committees; audit, compensation (or remuneration), and nomination committees. This is in line with best Corporate Governance practice.

The descriptions of how each committee functions, and its responsibilities, would appear to be appropriate.

However, given the (relatively small) number of NEDs, it may be difficult to run these committees effectively. In addition, the Audit Committee should have one NED with financial experience. As we do not have the background to the NEDs we do not know whether this criteria can be met.

Overall

Fizz has been in existence since 1890 and, despite recent poor financial figures, there is no information to suggest that there are concerns over how the company is run. However, Fizz does not appear to have the right structure in place in order to provide the "checks and balances" to ensure that governance issues do not arise in the future that may jeopardise the company's performance.

4   Discuss Fizz's exposure to currency risk.

Translation risk

Currency risk of holding foreign assets or liabilities.

Fizz does not yet hold any foreign assets or liabilities, therefore has no translation risk.

Although Joocy Juice is made using fruit that is processed close to source, Fizz does not own any of the land or processing plants.

Translation risk does not tend to be mitigated by companies as it does not represent a real loss/gain of cash but is a "book entry".

Transaction risk

This is the risk of buying and selling on credit in foreign currency.

Transaction risk is can be significant for Fizz (though it should be remembered the risk may be upside as well as downside).

For instance, Fizz has outsourced suppliers and also buys commodities from abroad. These are currently evaluated in the risk register with a score of 20 out of possible 25, therefore the company sees this risk as high.

Fizz may use a mixture of internal and external hedging. Internal methods are arranged by Fizz itself whereas external methods would use an exchange or bank.

Internal methods may include simply pay early or as late as possible. This is known as "leading and lagging". Its effectiveness depends on the ability to predict the exchange rate, however. Netting is another popular form of internal hedging, however it may be limited in Fizz's case. It depends on there being an offsetting foreign receipt to net off against a payment. Fizz's exports are limited at the moment therefore the likelihood of foreign currency income is low. Finally, Fizz may be able to deal with all suppliers in its home currency of N\$. This will depend on its bargaining power however. Fizz may have to accept a higher price from such suppliers who may seek compensation for having to take the exchange rate risk. It would also mean that Fizz may not benefit from any upside in the exchange rate.

The most popular method of external hedging is using forward contracts. This would allow Fizz to fix the exchange rate that it would use in the future. It would give complete certainty over the payment Fizz would have to pay, however it would take away any upside potential.

Fizz could also simply exchange money into currency required, open a bank account in that currency and earn interest in that account until the payment is due. This is a called a money market hedge (MMH). It takes away currency risk as the exchange is done immediately. Many companies will hold cash in a foreign bank account if that currency is used very often for convenience. (And it can help with internal netting arrangements although these opportunities may be limited for Fizz, as stated above).

Fizz could use an exchange to set up futures or options. Futures are similar to forward contracts as they enable Fizz to fix the future value of a transaction. However, by doing so, just as with forward contracts, Fizz would not be able to take advantage of any upside change to the exchange rate. Taking out an option *would* allow Fizz to choose between the results offered by using the option or instead Fizz could use the prevailing market exchange rate - which means the best result for Fizz would be chosen. Though this is advantageous, options are the most expensive form of hedging.

Economic risk

Whereas with transaction risk, the invoice amount for payment/receipt is known, economic risk covers the long term currency exposure Fizz may have due to its global presence.

For instance, let's say that Fizz has regular supplier payments to make in US$ as it has a contract with an aluminium supplier. It expects to have to pay these for 3 years, although the amount is not fixed for the three year term. Fizz knows that it will have to exchange N$ into US$, however, it does not know what the long term currency movement may be (is the N$ likely to appreciate/depreciate?). Nor does it know exactly what the amount may be in future years (which makes it difficult to hedge). This form of currency risk is known as economic risk.

Economic risk can also affect Fizz in another way: competitiveness. It may set prices for products in advance based on costs of production and a mark-up. The costs may be increasing due to exchange rate changes and therefore payments to suppliers, so Fizz would also like to increase its retail prices. Competitors that are dealing with suppliers and currencies less affected by exchange rates may be able to charge less. Fizz may need to reduce margins in order to compete.

Economic risk is difficult to hedge as the exact sums are not known. With transaction risk, the sum is known as there is a specific receipt or payment and a suitable hedging product can be sought. The sums involved with economic risk are more vague and long term, therefore internal hedging is generally more effective, especially netting. However the opportunity for netting at Fizz is limited.

Economic risk can be mitigated through diversification. Fizz has already got a diversified portfolio therefore not all its drinks rely on, say, aluminium and therefore are affected by this commodity price. It may also diversify its supply so that not all aluminium comes from the US and therefore needs to be paid in US$.

Economic risk can also be mitigated through creating a strong brand. Any increases in commodity prices can be passed onto customers as they are willing to pay an increased price for that drink. That is, the product is "price inelastic". This effect may be limited to Fizz and competition may be very strong and customers not necessarily loyal to a particular brand.

5   Identify possible strategies for growth for Fizz.

In order to consider the ways in which Fizz might grow, use will be made of Ansoff's matrix, which looks at two different variables for growth – the products that are offered, and the markets that are served. Both of these can be addressed under the headings of 'Existing' and 'New'

Market Penetration (Existing Product, Existing Market)

This is an exercise in trying to achieve growth through increasing current market share. For Fizz, this means selling more soft drinks in the markets in which it is already present.

There are a number of ways in which such growth in market share can be achieved. Firstly, there could be considered investment in drinks that are already manufactured by Fizz. Expenditure on advertising might cause existing customers to purchase Fizz products in greater quantities, or alternatively attract new customers in Nortland to switch from buying competitor products. This would certainly have a positive effect on reported revenues.

However, a detailed analysis of how profits would be affected would need to be carried out first. Advertising can be an expensive exercise, and Fizz must be confident that the benefits would outweigh the extra costs.

Profits could also be increased through a cost cutting exercise. This would also fit under the heading of market penetration; the company isn't necessarily doing anything different, it is simply operating more efficiently. Value analysis should be conducted throughout the Fizz supply and manufacturing chains to identify costs that can be reduced or eliminated.

A further market penetration strategy would be to acquire another business that operates in Fizz's market and sells competing goods. In effect, Fizz would acquire the sales that the rival is currently enjoying, adding to market share and revenues, and should also be able to produce synergies such as cost savings, thereby improving profitability. The difficulty comes in identifying a suitable target and agreeing a value that represents a good deal for Fizz.

Product Development (Existing Market, New Product)

In the case of Fizz, adopting a Product Development strategy would mean introducing new types of soft drinks into the markets in which it already sells. For example, the company could start making products such as smoothies and other milk-based drinks, or flavoured mineral waters.

For such a strategy to be successful, Fizz would need to focus carefully on both market research and research and development. The ideal would be to identify a market need that has good growth potential and is not yet being satisfied, and then to formulate a product that meets the demands of consumers.

The product needn't be something completely different, it could simply be a new version of an existing product. For example, a new variant of Joocy Juice which contains less sugar could be formulated to combat concerns consumers may have over the health benefits of the existing recipe.

Market Development (Existing Product, New Market)

A strategy of market development would mean either identifying new countries into which Fizz could sell its products, or targeting new consumer segments that perhaps are not currently buying Fizz products.

In terms of geography, the company should look to enter markets that show good growth potential both now and into the future. For example, emerging economies such as India and China are likely to see growing levels of consumer income and a demand for products accepted as 'the norm' in more established economies.

For example, Fizz's oldest product Froot is very well-established and may well have great sales potential abroad. Fizz should identify suitable target markets, and then determine the most appropriate way in which to enter those markets. This might mean simply increasing production in Nortland and then exporting. Alternatively, it might be more appropriate to enter a franchise arrangement with a local soft drinks company, much as Qwench has done in the cola market. As its competitor has proved, such agreements can add significantly to revenues whilst the chosen franchisee carries out much of the work to earn profits.

Alternatively, market development could involve targeting new consumer groups that currently are not included within the typical Fizz customer profile. For example, the energy drink Funn is deliberately targeted at teenagers and people in their early 20s. The product itself, being high energy, together with the very name of the drink, is deliberately aimed at the fast-living, thrill-seeking consumer. However, a variation of the same recipe but with a different marketing message could be targeted at a completely different type of customer, say the executive who works long hours and needs a boost at certain points in his/her working day. Or the young parent, sleep-deprived due to the regular demands of their child during the night, who needs something to kick-start the system before they can function properly.

Diversification (New Product, New Market)

This growth strategy carries the greatest degree of risk, as invariably every aspect of it is new, both the product and the market. For example, Fizz could move into making alcoholic drinks, snack foods or any other area of industry – all would fit under this heading on the model.

Diversification can be further analysed under the headings of related or unrelated. Related diversification occurs where a business stays within the same area of industry, but moves up/down or across the supply chain. For example, Fizz could integrate backwards up its supply chain ("vertical integration") by buying a corn syrup farm and starting to make for itself its raw material requirements instead of relying on third party suppliers.

Alternatively, moving into making alcoholic drinks would require many of the current skills (production, bottling, distribution, marketing etc.) but would represent a significant shift away from soft drinks into a completely different area of the food and drink industry.

Alternatively, Fizz could grow by moving away from drinks manufacturing as part of its new strategy – for example, publishing recipe books based on the drinks Fizz makes, as non-alcoholic cocktails are growing in popularity (publishing is a very different discipline); or creating a range of snacks, aimed at those who like to eat and drink at the same time. Indeed, this form of unrelated diversification is without limit – anything is (theoretically) possible.

Organic Growth/ Acquisition/Collaboration

Another way of looking at the possibilities for growth is to consider whether it should be done by organic means (e.g. Fizz adds further drinks to its portfolio); or whether it should be done by means of a merger or acquisition (e.g. buying or merging with another business, such as Qwench).

Both approaches have their relative advantages and disadvantages. For example, organic growth tends to be slower – if Fizz were to wish to introduce new drinks into its portfolio, it would take considerable time to develop the idea, find the right blend of ingredients, create the appropriate brand and marketing message etc. Achieving a tie-up with a company such as Qwench or a franchise deal with other drinks manufacturers could significantly increase the sales channels that Fizz operates in at a faster rate, whilst sharing the risks of expansion with other parties. However, Fizz would also need to share the rewards, and also questions exist over quality control and the desire to remain independent.

Exercise 2 – Fizz: Ratio Analysis

Ratio Analysis	Fizz		Qwench	
	2018	**2017**	**2018**	**2017**
Capital employed				
Equity	272.8	237.6	983.1	728.3
Debt	21.3	10.4	340.0	386.3
Total	294.1	248.0	1,323.1	1,114.6
Statement of profit or loss (extracts)				
Revenue	336.2	365.3	1,690.1	1,882.2
Operating profit	75.8	97.4	332.5	448.3
Finance costs	(1.1)	(0.4)	(27.2)	(30.9)
Profit after tax	66.0	86.7	262.4	380.9
Return on capital employed:	25.8%	39.3%	25.1%	40.2%
(operating profit / capital employed)				
Operating profit margin:	22.5%	26.7%	19.7%	23.8%
(operating profit / revenue)				
Asset turnover:	1.14	1.47	1.28	1.69
(revenue / capital employed)				
Return on equity:	24.2%	36.5%	26.7%	52.3%
(profit after tax / equity)				
Gearing:	7.24%	4.19%	25.70%	34.66%
(debt / debt + equity)				

Commentary:

Both companies have seen a distinct decline in their performance ratios (gearing excluded), but there are some interesting differences.

Return on capital employed (ROCE) is virtually identical for both companies in both years, but looking behind that we see that Fizz has a consistently higher operating profit margin than Qwench but a consistently lower Asset turnover. It appears that Fizz is better at turning revenue into profit but not as good at generating the revenue from its available capital. (In 2016 Fizz generated just N$1.14 of revenue from each N$ invested in the business, compared to Qwench at N$1.28 of revenue per N$ invested.)

Whilst both companies have seen an almost identical fall in ROCE, Fizz has seen a much smaller decline in Return on Equity. (Qwench's Return on equity has almost halved whereas Fizz's has dropped by just one third.) This difference is likely to be due, at least in part, to the much lower level of gearing in Fizz than in Qwench.

Exercise 3 – Fizz: SWOT analysis

Strengths

- Quoted company status, meaning that fresh finance can be raised if needed

- Well-established company that is over 100 years old, therefore has track record that will give customers/suppliers/financiers confidence

- Diversified range of products, reducing risk of business failure

- All operations take place on one site, making management easier

- Functional structure, allowing for clear management responsibility

- Clear use of branding for products aimed at particular market segments

- Low level of financial gearing

- Diversified sales channels (on-trade and off-trade)

- Joocy Juice – visible differentiating features compared to competitor products)

- Relatively strong share price performance (when compared to main competitor)

Weaknesses

- Declining financial performance in 2016 v 2015

- Little business diversification (only involved in soft drinks)

- Possible accusation of inappropriate governance (not equal split between EDs/NEDs)

- Low asset turnover ratio compared to Qwench

Opportunities

- International expansion – licencing, franchising, construct overseas facility etc.

- Franchise arrangements to sell other manufacturers' products in Nortland (as Qwench does)

- Expand mineral water product as market demand is growing

- Growth by acquisition (could fund through share issue/debt)

Threats

- Possibility of hostile takeover

- Government legislation against high calorie drinks (so-called 'sugar tax')

- Consumer protests that damage Fizz name (against 'unhealthy' drinks) e.g. "Fighting Fat"

- Risk of inaccurate labelling of product ingredients

- Problems in the production process e.g. contamination

- Failure in supply chain – some product shipped straight to customers by third parties

- Rise in raw material prices (most raw materials are commodities, therefore price determined by the market)

- Failure of IT systems

- 'Copycat' producers who infringe Fizz intellectual property

- Change in consumer patterns e.g. customers move away from sugar drinks due to increasing health awareness

Exam day techniques

Chapter learning objectives

- To develop a carefully planned and thought through strategy to cope with the three hours of exam time

1 Exam day strategy

Once you have studied the pre-seen, learnt the three subject syllabi thoroughly and practised lots of exercises and mocks, you should be well prepared for the exam.

However, it is still important to have a carefully planned and thought through strategy to cope with those three hours of exam time.

This chapter takes you through some of the key skills to master to ensure all your careful preparation does not go to waste.

2 Importance of time management

Someone once referred to case study exams as "the race against time" and it's difficult to imagine a more accurate description. Being able to do what the examiner is wanting is only half of the battle; being able to deliver it in the time available is another matter altogether. This is even more important than in previous exams you may have faced because each section in the real exam is now timed and that once that time is up you will be moved on. Case study is not like a traditional exam where you can go back to a question if you get extra inspiration or feel you have some time left over. You have to complete each task within the time stated.

For this reason, time management is a key skill required to pass the Case Study Examination.

Successful time management requires two things:

- A tailored time plan – one that plays to your personal strengths and weaknesses; and

- Discipline in order to stick to it!

Time robbers

There are a number of ways in which time can be wasted or not used effectively in the Case Study Examination. An awareness of these will help to ensure you don't waste time in your exam.

Inactive reading

The first part of each task must be spent actively reading, processing the information and considering the impact on the organisation, how the issues link together and what could be done to resolve them. You may not have time to have a second detailed read and so these thoughts must be captured first time around.

Too much time spent on presentation

You will be writing your answer in software with some similarities to Microsoft Word however the only functions available are

- Cut
- Copy
- Paste
- Undo
- Redo
- Bold
- Italic
- Underline

The temptation to make various words bold or italics or underlined, is very hard to resist. But, resist you must! There are little, if any, marks available for having a response that is well presented, and these finer details will be worth nothing at all. Good presentation could involve writing in paragraphs, which makes the progression from one line of thought to the next much easier and subheadings within answers. CIMA wouldn't actually award marks for that, but a well-structured argument demonstrates greater understanding.

Being a perfectionist

Students can often spend such a long time pondering about what to write that over the course of a 3 hour exam, over half of it is spent staring into space.

As you are sitting a computer exam you not only spend time pondering, but also have the ability to delete so can change your mind several times before settling on the right word combinations. Just focus on getting your points down and don't worry about whether they could have been phrased better.

Although do bear in mind that the marker has to be able to read and understand your answer, so do write in clear English.

Too much detail on earlier parts of the requirement

As we've said earlier, not finishing answers is a key reason for failing the Case Study Examination. One of the main reasons why students fail to finish a section is a lack of discipline when writing about an issue. They feel they have to get all of their points down rather than selecting the better points and moving on. If a task requires you to discuss three different areas it is vital that you cover all parts adequately.

Too much correction

Often students can reread paragraphs three or more times before they move on to writing the next part of their answer. Instead, try to leave the read through until the final few minutes of the task and try to correct as many obvious errors as possible. The CIMA marker will be reading and marking your script on screen and it is harder to read and understand the points you are making if there are many typing errors.

3 Assimilation of information

One of the most challenging things to deal with in a case study examination is the volume of information which you have available. This is particularly difficult when you have both pre-seen and unseen information to manage and draw from. It is important that you refer to relevant pre-seen information in your responses as well as incorporating the unseen information.

The key things that you need to do to assimilate the information effectively and efficiently are:

- Read about and identify each event

- Consider what the issue is

- Evaluate the impact of the issue. Who is affected, by how much are they affected and what would happen if no action was taken?

- Determine the most useful and relevant exhibits from the pre-seen

Capturing all of your thoughts and ideas at this stage can be difficult and time consuming.

The following section on planning your answer will show you how to do this effectively without wasting time or effort.

4 Planning your answers

In section 2 of this chapter we saw how important it was to manage your time in the exam to ensure you're able to complete all of the necessary stages in the preparation of your answer.

One important aspect of your exam is planning your answer. Sitting the Case Study Exam is not as straight forward as turning up, reading the requirements, and then writing your answer.

If you do attempt to write without any form of content plan, your response will lack direction and a logical flow, it won't fully address the key points required and any recommendations will lack solid justification. It is for this reason that time should be specifically allocated to planning the content of your answers.

Given the preparation you've done before the exam, reading the unseen can often feel like a firework display is happening in your brain; each new piece of information you read about triggers a series of thoughts and ideas.

The planning process must therefore begin as soon as you start reading the unseen information. Every second counts within the case study exam and so it's important to use all of your time effectively by capturing the thoughts as they come to you.

To make sure the time spent now is of use to you throughout the task, you will need to consider carefully how best to document your thoughts. You will be provided with an on-screen notes page ('scratchpad') as well as a wipe-clean laminated notes page and marker pen. Any method you adopt to plan must be concise whilst still allowing you to capture all of your ideas and see the bigger picture in terms of how the issues interrelate with one another (see additional guidance below). Furthermore, the method must suit you! Everyone is different and what might work for one person could be a disaster for another. For example, some people prefer to work with lists, others with mind maps.

Most people find that some form of central planning sheet (to enable the bigger picture to be seen) is best. How you prepare the central planning sheet is a matter of personal preference and we've given illustrations of two different methods below. Practise each one to find out which you prefer and then tailor it further to settle on something that works for you.

Method 1 – The ordered list

This process is ideally suited to people who prefer lists and structure.

Step 1:

- Begin by reading everything in the task exhibit
- Ensure you have identified all aspects of the task and then write this on the left hand side of your planning sheet

Step 2:

- Read everything in the trigger exhibit, making notes next to the relevant task

Step 3:

- Review your list to identify any linkages to information provided in the pre-seen and note next to the task on your planning sheet

Step 4:

- Brainstorm any technical knowledge you can use in responding to the task and note this on your planning sheet

Illustration 1 – Planning

On Monday morning your boss arrived in work full of enthusiasm for a new business venture he had thought of over the weekend. This was in response to a conversation that had taken place at Friday night drinks when the CEO expressed concern that she felt the business was stagnating and needed some new products to rekindle customer interest.

Your boss needed to harness his ideas and put together an outline plan for a mid-morning coffee meeting with the CEO. Typically, the idea had germinated without sufficient thought and you were asked to consider the critical factors that needed to be considered in launching the new product and write a briefing document for the meeting.

Requirement:

Prepare a plan for your briefing document.

Solution

Critical factors	Goals and objectives	Skills and experience	Finance	Marketing and sales
New product	Matches mission and objectives?	Experience in manufacturing?	Available finance?	Advertising
	Strengths?	Available labour?	Investment?	Social media
			Working capital?	Website?
Technical content?		SAF?	Debt v equity? Investment appraisal techniques?	

Method 2 – The extended mind map

This process is ideally suited to those who prefer pictures and diagrams to trigger their thoughts.

Step 1:

- Read the unseen information and identify the key tasks required

- As you read, write each task in a "bubble" on your planning sheet.

Step 2:

- Keep adding each new part of the task you identify to your sheet. At the end you should have a page with a number of bubbles dotted about.

Step 3:

- Review your bubbles to identify any linkages to the trigger information or pre-seen exhibits. Add any relevant information to your planning sheet in a bubble attached to the appropriate part of the task.

Step 4:

- Review the task bubbles and brainstorm any relevant knowledge which you can use in responding to the task. Add this to bubbles attached to the task.

With detailed information provided in the exam it would be very likely that your brain would think of a wide range of ideas which, if left uncaptured, would be forgotten as quickly as you thought of them.

This is where mind mapping comes in handy. You would not of course need to draw one as neat as this and feel free to add colours or graphics to help your thought processes.

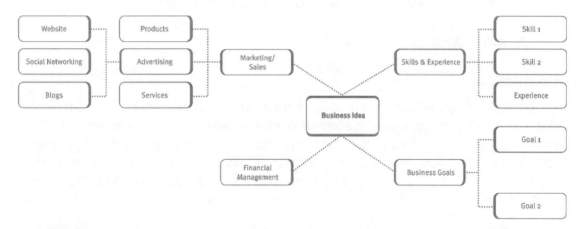

Have a go!

Why not try putting your thoughts on the previous illustration into a mind map like the one above?

Some additional guidance

(1) This is perhaps the hardest part of the exam; as soon as you tell your brain it needs to come up with some ideas, it very often refuses to cooperate! Practice makes perfect so working through the exercises in Chapter 7 and attempting mock exams will really help your brain to deliver ideas when you need it to.

(2) Don't simply view technical models as something that must be included to tick a box if explicitly requested in the requirements. Instead use the models to help analyse the issues, suggest solutions or generate ideas. They were developed to be useful!

(3) If you start looking at one of the task requirements and are stuck for ideas, don't waste time staring into space. Move on to the next part of the task (but not onto the next task itself as you won't be able to return) and you'll find the creative juices soon start flowing.

5 Communication skills

The Case Study examinations aim to test a wide range of skills and you may be required to communicate in many different ways to various different audiences, each with different information needs. How well you communicate will be directly linked to the marks earned – clear, appropriate communication will always score better than confused, irrelevant or vague ideas.

In Strategic Case study, the examiners do not tend to ask for specific formats for a response – an email, letter, report etc. Instead, you should simply type your answer in the box provided, getting straight into the answer to the instructions set, as if you were typing out the body of a report.

6 Writing style

Introduction

Writing style is something that develops over time. It is influenced by your education and experiences. To some it comes easily, they enjoy words – but remember, you are not looking to win any prizes in literature. It's about putting facts, ideas and opinions in a clear, concise, logical fashion. Some students get very worried about their writing styles. As a general rule you should try to write as you would talk.

Logical flow

A typical point starts with a statement of fact, either given in the case or derived from analysis – 'what?'

This can then be followed by an interpretation – 'so what?'

This can then lead to an implication – 'now what?', or 'what next?'

For example:

(1)   What? – The net relevant cash flow for the project is positive.

(2)   So what? – Suggesting we should go ahead with the project.

(3)   Now what? – Arrange board meeting to discuss strategic implications.

A similar structure can be obtained using the Socratic approach – what, why, how?

- So what?

- Why should we use it?

- How does it work?

Who is reading the response?

Failure to pitch the level correctly will inevitably result in failure to communicate your ideas effectively, since the reader will either be swamped with complexity, or bored with blandness. The recipients of the report should also dictate the level of tact required.

Tactless	Tactful
The directors have clearly made errors	There were other options open to the board that, with hindsight, would have been beneficial
The marketing director is responsible for this disastrous change in strategy	The board should consider where this went wrong? It would appear that the marketing department may have made some mistakes

This has to be considered carefully. If, for argument's sake, the question asked for an evaluation of a director's proposal, it would cost marks if the candidate glossed over the proposal's weaknesses in order to avoid upsetting the Boss. The "real world" analogy can be taken too far.

It should be made clear that candidates will never be penalised for rejecting or disagreeing with a proposal made by the CEO or any other senior colleague if doing so results in a strong and relevant answer to the requirement.

Making your response easy to read

To ensure that the marker finds your answers accessible and easy to read, you should try to do the following:

- Use short words, short sentences, short phrases and short paragraphs. If you are adopting the 'what, so what, what now' approach, then you could have a paragraph containing three sentences. The next point can then be a new paragraph, also containing three sentences.

- Use the correct words to explain what you mean! For example, students often get confused between:

    - recommendations (what they should do – actions) and options (what they could do – possibilities).

    - objectives (what we want to achieve – the destination) and strategies (how we intend to achieve them – the route).

- Avoid using vague generalisations. Too often students will comment that an issue will "impact" on profit rather than being specific about whether profit will increase or decrease (or even better still, trying to quantify by how much). Other common phrases which are too vague include "communicate with" (you need to say specifically what should be discussed) and "look in to" (how should an option be looked in to?)

- Avoid unnecessary repetition. This can either be of information from the exam paper (pre-seen or unseen), of discussion within the report (in particular between what is said in one section and another) or can relate to the words that you use. Some students fall into the trap of thinking that writing a professional report means simply writing more words to say the same thing! The issue is quality not quantity.

    For example, compare the following:

    - 'I, myself, personally' OR 'I'

    - 'export overseas' OR 'export'

    - 'green in colour' OR 'green'

- Watch your spelling – this may seem a small and unimportant point, but poor spelling makes a document seem sloppy and may convey an impression that the content is as loose as the general appearance! Having said this, do not worry about the occasional spelling mistake or typo in your answer; CIMA will not penalise you, provided they can understand what you are trying to say.

- Recommendations – be decisive – do not 'sit on the fence' or ask for more information. Make a clear recommendation based on the information you have and justify why you have chosen that course of action.

Exercise 1

This exercise will get you thinking about what makes a well written script. The technical content of the requirement is not relevant – we are focusing on writing style and flow.

The risk committee of X plc met to discuss a report by its risk manager. The report focused on a number of risks that applied to a chemicals factory recently acquired in another country.

She explained that the new risks related to the security of the new factory in respect of burglary, the supply of one of the key raw materials that experienced fluctuations in world supply and also an environmental risk.

The environmental risk was with respect to the possibility of poisonous emissions from the new factory. The CEO who chaired the risk committee, said that the factory was important to him for two reasons. First, he said it was strategically important to the company. Second, it was important because his own bonuses depended upon it. He said that he knew from the report what the risks were, but that he wanted somebody to explain to him what strategies they could use to manage the risks. 'I don't get any bonus at all until we reach a high level of output from the factory,' he said. 'So I don't care what the risks are, we will have to manage them.'

You have been asked to outline strategies that can be used to manage risk and identify, with reasons, an appropriate strategy for each of the three risks facing the new venture.

Requirement:

Consider these two responses and note the positive and negative aspects of each.

Answer 1

Introduction

Risk can be managed using the following strategies.

- **Transfer** the risk to another organisation for example by buying insurance. This is usually cost effective where the probability of the risk is low but the impact is potentially high.

- **Avoid** the risk altogether by withdrawing completely from the risky activity. This is done where the risk is high probability and high frequency and so it is too costly to reduce the risk sufficiently.

- **Reduce** the risk by implementing controls or by diversification.

- **Accept** the risk without taking any further steps to mitigate it. For this to be acceptable the frequency and the impact of the risk must place the risk within the risk appetite of the company.

Risk of burglary

It is usual to insure against burglary an example of the transfer strategy. This is because of the high impact of burglary.

It is also usual to put safeguards in place such as security guards because of the probability of burglary. This is an example of risk reduction.

Raw materials supply fluctuation

Depending on the cost benefit analysis the company could chose to transfer the risk by entering into forward contracts to purchase the materials.

There will be a cost associated with this and it will lower but not remove the risk associated with supply and price fluctuations. They may choose to accept the risk as part of the operational risk associated with their industry.

Environmental risk

The company should take reasonable steps to reduce the chance poisonous emissions. It should use appropriate technology and controls to reduce the risk.

Risks cannot be completely eliminated so if the poisonous emissions could give rise to significant costs it should also purchase insurance and transfer the risk.

Answer 2

Risk is managed by this:

(1) Identify the risk. This is by brainstorming all the things that the risk can be.

(2) Risk assessment. We won't know this properly until afterwards.

(3) Risk Profiling. This is decided on consequences and impact.

(4) Risk quantification. This can be average loss or it can be largest loss.

(5) Risk consolidation which will depend on the risk appetite and diversification.

The risks at the factory are:

- The main risk at the factory is environmental risk. You can't do anything about this risk because global warming is because of everyone.

- The big risk is that the CEO is "I don't care what the risks are" this will need to have the risk awareness embedded in and the tone at the top.

- The other risk is that the CEO could manipulate the output levels to get his bonus. This needs to be looked at seriously because he is also on the risk committee and the remuneration committee and he is not independent and that should be a NED.

7 Summary

You should have an appreciation of some of the issues you may encounter in the exam and some possible techniques to overcome these.

Next steps:

(1) In the next two chapters we will present the unseen and guide you through the process of producing an answer. It is worth ensuring you can log on to the Pearson Vue site now and make sure you have registered for the practice case study exam. It is advisable to familiarise yourself with the software as much as possible.

(2) As you are about to embark on a full attempt at the question tutorial exam it is a good time to revisit previous chapters and ensure you are comfortable with all of the material so far before proceeding.

Test your understanding answers

Exercise 1

The first solution has several positive aspects:

- Brief introduction linking to requirement
- Overview of model with explanation and clear examples
- Specific points from scenario addressed
- Headings clearly signpost the answer
- Appropriate language

There are some areas which could be improved:

- Specific reference to the company name
- More explicit use of the information from the scenario

The second solution is not as strong as the first. Some of the main criticisms:

- Main options available are not clearly explained
- No attempt to introduce the answer
- Inappropriate language for a formal report/response
- Lack of tact regarding the CEO – the intended audience!!

As a piece of writing there is not much to say from a positive perspective except:

- Clear structure
- Writing is concise (but probably a bit too brief)

Prototype exam variant 1 – walkthrough

Chapter learning objectives

- To gain experience trying to answer a case study exam.

1   The aim of a walkthrough

The aim of this chapter is to give you a chance to practise many of the techniques you have been shown in previous chapters of this study text. This should help you to understand the various thought processes needed to complete the full three hour examination. It is important that you work through this chapter at a steady pace.

Don't rush on to the next stage until you have properly digested the information, followed the guidance labelled 'Stop and Think!' and made your own notes. This will give you more confidence than simply reading the model solutions. You should refer to the unseen produced in the previous chapter as you proceed through these exercises.

The following chapter will then guide you through the suggested solutions and marking key.

2   First screen

The opening screen of the exam shows you how many sub-tasks you have to deal with and how to allocate your time within tasks:

Section (task)	Time for section (minutes)	Number of answer screens	Number of sub-tasks	% time to spend on each sub-task
1	60	1	2	(a) 55% (b) 45%
2	60	1	2	(a) 55% (b) 45%
3	60	1	3	(a) 60% (b) 20% (c) 20%

The exam software will prevent you from spending more than 60 minutes on task 2, say, but you need to ensure that this is split 33 minutes on sub-task (a) and 27 minutes on sub-task (b)

3   Task 1

Understanding the context

The first screen of task 1 reveals that Fizz is concerned about the possible introduction of a sugar tax:

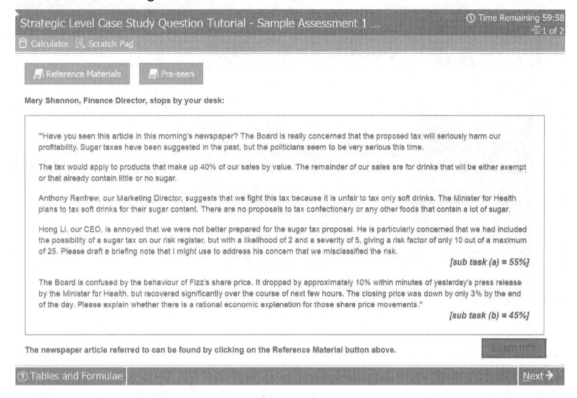

Stop and think!

(1)   Start thinking about the relevant information in the pre-seen. It's very important that your responses are applied to the scenario. For example, how much can you remember about the possibility of a sugar tax being introduced, and how it might impact on Fizz? We were told in the pre-seen that

"Governments are increasingly concerned about the rising costs of illnesses such as type 2 diabetes and cancer, which have risen alongside an obesity epidemic. The battle between food companies and governments may be only just beginning; if health systems fail under the strain of obesity-related diseases, regulators will act to prevent rather than treat them afterwards.

Several countries are introducing legislation to help curb intake of sugary foods; health warnings, sales taxes, banning of junk foods in schools, restrictions on advertising to children and reduced portion sizes may become more prevalent." *(Daily News article)*

(2)   Fizz has identified on its risk register that the company faces risk of legislation or tax penalties to discourage the sale of high calorie products.

(3)   The Board of Fizz is also committed to a strategy of developing consumer trust; its industry has been associated with a number of health scares in recent years and it recognises the need to develop both products and marketing strategies that can overcome such difficulties.

Answering the question set – understanding the detail and linking to the requirements

The detail in the issue is given in the reference materials:

It is vital that you understand the nature and scope of the requirements. Here you need to prepare a briefing note which covers the following:

- An explanation that will address the CEO's concern that, whilst the possible introduction of a sugar tax was included on the company's risk register, it had not been given a higher risk weighting

  Make sure you answer the question set – do not talk in just general terms about a risk register. You need to focus on this risk in particular and the nature of Fizz's business model. In this case, the issue is that the risk had to be classified in terms of what was known and understood at the time. The fact that the risk has subsequently increased does not necessarily mean that the earlier classification was wrong.

- Explain to the Board whether there is a rational economic explanation over the company's share price movements following the government announcement.

  "To **explain**" is a higher level verb that "to list". You need to make clear further details about the share price movements – introduce the theory of how shares are valued, why this might rise and fall, and then apply it to these particular circumstances (including mention of practical/non-theoretical issues).

Let's plan – Task 1(a)

If you prefer to plan within your answer box, then the above considerations will help you set up suitable headings and then start to populate them.

Alternatively, if you prefer to use your wipe clean whiteboard, then you could split your planning sheet into a grid to ensure all parts are covered:

Idea	Comments
General comments on risk registers	
Comments specific to Fizz	

Either way, you now need to brainstorm all the relevant points you can think of under the above headings, making sure you are bringing together your knowledge from the relevant syllabus as well as your analysis of the pre-seen information.

Let's think a bit more about these requirements by breaking them down into the component parts.

Risk registers – from your P3 studies you will know that compiling a risk register is a matter of judgement. Different people can view each risk that the organisation faces in a different way when it comes to assessing likelihood or impact. Furthermore, a risk register needs to be reviewed on a regular basis and updated if necessary.

Specific comments – this announcement from the government might be the result of a new political initiative, one that perhaps has only just come about because of a change in political thinking or change in ruling party. It might also have been released just now to deflect criticism of the government due to its general healthcare policies, not just obesity or diabetes. In other words, the government is taking a populist step to deflect criticism from itself.

Task 1(b)

Again you could set up headings within your answer or use a planning sheet:

Ideas	Comments
General theory on share price valuation	
Practical influences on share prices	

From your F3 knowledge, you will be aware that there is much theory on how shares are valued – for example, efficient market hypothesis theory. This can be used to introduce an understanding of why prices change.

On the other hand, you will also be aware of other, real-world impacts on share price moves e.g. short term speculators, time taken to digest new information that has been released to the market.

Try to focus on both of the above determinants of share value, remembering to make your comments as specific to Fizz and the threat of a new tax as possible.

As a rough rule of thumb you should spend about 15–20% of the time available for reading and planning. So for this section of the exam, where you are given 60 minutes, you should be spending approximately 9–12 minutes planning your answer before you complete the exercise below. This would leave you about 45–50 minutes to write your answer and perhaps a few minutes spare to check through what you have written.

Exercise 1

Prepare a response to the first task in the prototype exam Fizz.

4 Task 2

For task 2, the trigger and requirements are again mixed together into one screen, followed by reference material on a different screen:

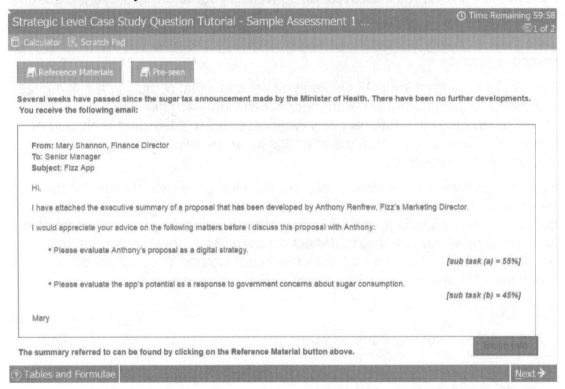

Understanding the context

With tasks like this, where there is little context given supporting the requirements, it is very important that you work carefully through the reference materials that accompany the instructions, so that you can tailor your ideas to the specific context in the question and not simply produce a generic answer.

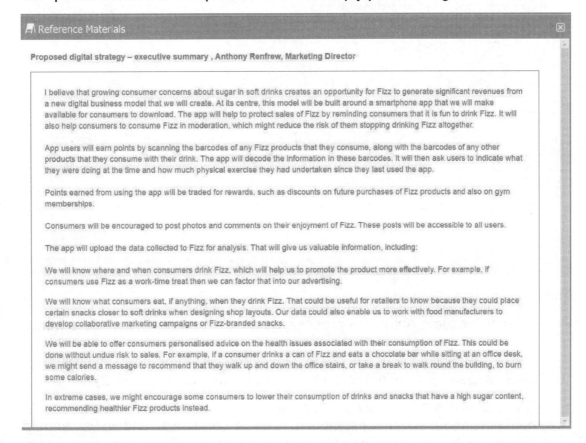

Reference Materials

Proposed digital strategy – executive summary , Anthony Renfrew, Marketing Director

I believe that growing consumer concerns about sugar in soft drinks creates an opportunity for Fizz to generate significant revenues from a new digital business model that we will create. At its centre, this model will be built around a smartphone app that we will make available for consumers to download. The app will help to protect sales of Fizz by reminding consumers that it is fun to drink Fizz. It will also help consumers to consume Fizz in moderation, which might reduce the risk of them stopping drinking Fizz altogether.

App users will earn points by scanning the barcodes of any Fizz products that they consume, along with the barcodes of any other products that they consume with their drink. The app will decode the information in these barcodes. It will then ask users to indicate what they were doing at the time and how much physical exercise they had undertaken since they last used the app.

Points earned from using the app will be traded for rewards, such as discounts on future purchases of Fizz products and also on gym memberships.

Consumers will be encouraged to post photos and comments on their enjoyment of Fizz. These posts will be accessible to all users.

The app will upload the data collected to Fizz for analysis. That will give us valuable information, including:

We will know where and when consumers drink Fizz, which will help us to promote the product more effectively. For example, if consumers use Fizz as a work-time treat then we can factor that into our advertising.

We will know what consumers eat, if anything, when they drink Fizz. That could be useful for retailers to know because they could place certain snacks closer to soft drinks when designing shop layouts. Our data could also enable us to work with food manufacturers to develop collaborative marketing campaigns or Fizz-branded snacks.

We will be able to offer consumers personalised advice on the health issues associated with their consumption of Fizz. This could be done without undue risk to sales. For example, if a consumer drinks a can of Fizz and eats a chocolate bar while sitting at an office desk, we might send a message to recommend that they walk up and down the office stairs, or take a break to walk round the building, to burn some calories.

In extreme cases, we might encourage some consumers to lower their consumption of drinks and snacks that have a high sugar content, recommending healthier Fizz products instead.

Stop and think!

(1) Is there any technical knowledge that might help you to answer the instructions? Of the three strategic papers, this seems most relevant to E3.

(2) What is the difference between the two instructions; at first glance, they seem very similar.

(3) What is your initial reaction to the proposal – does your 'gut feel' suggest that this is a good idea? Jot down initial thoughts

Answering the question set – understanding the requirements

In this instance, you are not requested to put your answer into any particular format; the answer box has already been set up for you to write an email to Mary Shannon, so you only have to focus on answering the instructions set! As indicated already, CIMA don't give marks for formatting. There wouldn't be a penalty for failing to set the document up as a letter, email, report or whatever.

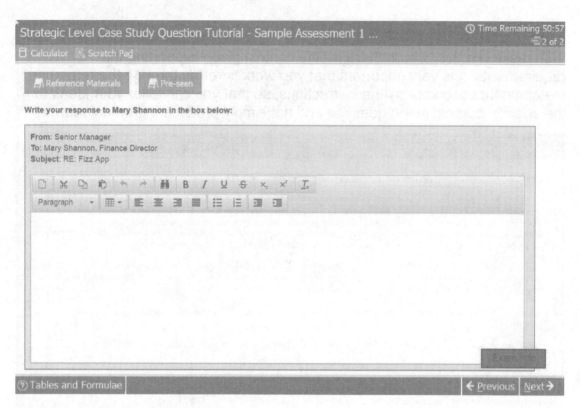

The precise instructions are:

- "Please evaluate Anthony's proposal as a digital strategy." As this is worth 55% of the marks for task 2, you should look to spend no more than 25 minutes on writing your answer to this instruction (remember, you will allow yourself 9-12 minutes to read and plan answers for task 2)

- "Please evaluate the app's potential as a response to government concerns about sugar consumption." This is worth 45%, and so you should aim to complete the writing of this answer in around 20 minutes.

Let's plan!

Task 2(a)

What does the instruction "evaluate" actually ask you to do? This is a high level verb (level 5 according to CIMA's verb hierarchy) and can be interpreted to mean "appraise or assess the value of". In short, it is asking for your opinion on the proposal, and wants advice as to whether it should be pursued or not.

There are a number of ways in which you could structure your answer to do this:

- Benefits and risks – highlight each under separate sub-headings, and then provide your conclusion.

- Advantages and disadvantages – same approach as above.

- Suitability/Feasibility/Acceptability – making use of the Johnson, Scholes and Whittington framework you studied at E3. The key here would be to conclude on each of SFA, and then provide an overall conclusion at the end.

Whatever technique you use to structure your answer, you must make sure that your ideas are relevant to Fizz, and not just a general appraisal of adopting some form of digital strategy.

Task 2(b)

This instruction also asks you to carry out an evaluation, but the focus is subtly different; you are now being asked to evaluate whether the app will potentially serve as a good response to the government concern over sugar consumption.

A suitable structure for your answer would appear to be:

- Identify reasons why you believe it would be a good response;

- Identify reasons why you believe it will not be a good response;

- End your answer with a conclusion – overall, do you think it will be viewed favourably as a response or not?

Exercise 2
Prepare a response to the second task.

5   Task 3

As for task 2, the trigger and requirements for task 3 are mixed together into one screen, together with reference material:

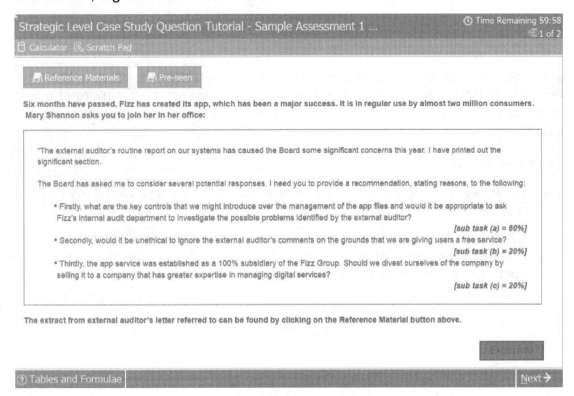

Understanding the context

After the appraisal that was conducted in task 2, it is clear that the decision was made by Fizz to develop the app; we are told that this has been met with great success. However, the reference materials highlight an issue brought to management's attention by the external auditor:

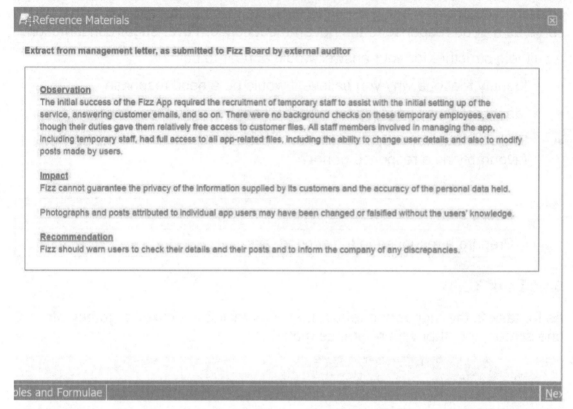

This issue is probably most relevant to the first 2 instructions for task 3; the failure to perform proper background checks on temporary staff is more of a short term issue, whereas the proposal in the third instruction is much more long term.

Stop and think!

- P3 would seem to provide the technical content for instruction 1 – what can you remember about controls and internal audit functions?

- E3 would seem to provide the background for instructions 2 and 3 (although, arguably, ethics is covered across all 3 strategic papers). Is such awareness likely to be of benefit to you?

Answering the question set – understanding the requirements

There would appear to be no set format for this task; the template provided, together with the instruction screen, does not specify an email, letter, report etc. You can simply write your ideas in the box provided:

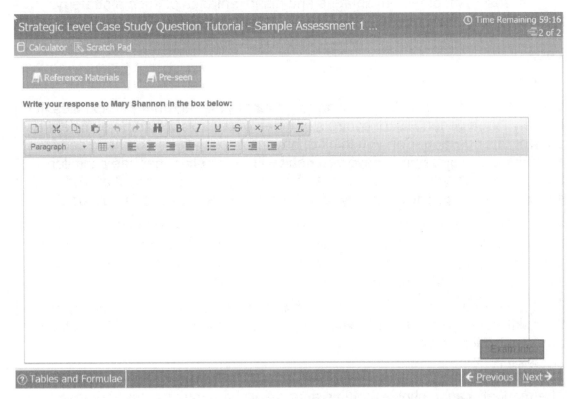

- Again, this task is allocated 60 minutes of time overall. You should spend 9-12 minutes reading and planning your answer to all 3 instructions, then allocate time to writing up your responses. This task has 3 separate instructions, so you will not be expected to spend as long on each one as in tasks 1 and 2. Instruction 1 is worth 60% of overall time, so writing your answer should take no longer than 27 minutes, with 9 minutes for instructions 2 and 3.

- Instruction 1 can be broken down into 2 parts – notice the use of the word 'and' in the middle. The first part is to suggest key controls that could be introduced over the management of the app files; this should be your first sub-heading to your answer.

  The second part is to question whether it would be appropriate to ask internal audit to investigate the possible problems identified by the external auditor. Again, it might be best to break this down into reasons why it would be appropriate, and reasons why it wouldn't, before finishing with a conclusion.

- Instruction 2 is asking for an assessment of whether a proposed action is ethical or not – can you think of an approach to dealing with such matters that you have studied at strategic level (or even before)?

- Instruction 3 is asking if Fizz should sell its new subsidiary – again, an assessment of the advantages and disadvantages of such a strategy, before giving a conclusion, is the best approach.

Let's plan!

Task 3(a)

The first instruction is asking for controls over the management of app files. It is unlikely that a generic list of controls or types of controls would be sufficient to answer this question. Can you think of any instances where you have seen something similar before? Have you dealt with a question that has a similar theme? Or have you had experience of working on an app project at work? If so, what are the practical ideas you can introduce to answer this question?

Also, go back to what data the app is looking to capture and the functionality that it has (reread the reference materials from task 2 if you need to. Does this give any inspiration for ideas? Can you think of how there might be control weaknesses with the app, and then use this as a source of ideas?

For the second instruction, ask yourself what internal auditors do? What are their skills and typical duties? What purpose does the internal audit function of an organisation serve?

Task 3(b)

The mark allocation shows that this answer will be relatively short compared to the other instructions you have addressed so far in this case study – do not feel under pressure to write a huge amount of content!

Think back to the fundamental ethical principles: integrity, objectivity, confidentiality, due professional behaviour, and professional competence. Does the suggestion to ignore the comments of the external auditor conflict with any of these?

Task 3(c)

As with the previous instruction, you do not have to write huge amounts here. Be practical in your advice – consider the long term strategy of Fizz, the very short time frame that it has had this subsidiary, the likely value that would be attributed to it, etc.

Exercise 3
Prepare a response to the third task.

6 Summary

You should now have a better understanding of how to approach the exam requirements and plan your answer. Although this chapter uses the pilot exam as an example, the techniques used can be applied to any set of exam tasks.

Next steps:

(1) As previously mentioned, you should attempt a written answer yourself to all of the tasks before reviewing the suggested solutions.

(2) Reviewing the solutions may highlight knowledge gaps which you may need to revisit.

(3) CIMA have produced two sample exams based on this pre-seen. You should try to attempt the second one at exam speed and using the exam software if possible.

Test your understanding answers

> *These answers have been provided by CIMA for information purposes only. The answers created are indicative of a response that could be given by a good candidate. They are not to be considered exhaustive, and other appropriate relevant responses would receive credit.*
>
> *CIMA will not accept challenges to these answers on the basis of academic judgement.*

Exercise 1

Requirement 1 – risk register

The whole point of the risk register is to ensure that risks are kept under observation and are managed appropriately. We need to be realistic about both the risk and the severity in order to do so. If we rate every risk as high then we will waste resources on observing and managing risks that are unlikely to occur. Every risk that is listed must, by definition, have a chance of occurring, otherwise it should not be on the register.

Thus, every risk classed as a probability of 1 or 2 could occur, even though such an event would effectively be unexpected.

The fact that the likelihood was classified as relatively low does not mean that it was not going to occur, merely that the probability was not deemed to be high. If the criticism is allowed to stand then Hong Li is effectively complaining that managers cannot predict the future, which is an unrealistic expectation. The danger is that managers may classify all risks as high in order to avoid such criticisms in the future and that could undermine the usefulness of the risk register by flagging too many risks as likely.

The fact that we rated the likelihood at 2/5 could have been an accurate reflection of the information that was available to us at the time. We can only determine why the tax was given such a low probability if we revisit the information that was available to us at the time with regard to the government's intentions during the period leading up to the announcement. We might reassure Hong by explaining where the evaluation of the probability came from. We might also show that the risks had been reviewed reasonably recently in order to reassure Hong that risks are kept under constant review.

On a related note, the question of when the entry was last updated would also be worth exploring. Managers should not be criticised for failing to predict adverse events, but they can be expected to respond to news and fresh information as and when it becomes available. Hong Li would be justified in complaining if the register had been allowed to become out of date.

It is worth pointing out that the nature of both the food industry and of politics means that there will be a constant threat of adverse legislation. The government may wish to demonstrate its concern about public health and may target almost any sector of the food industry in order to do so. The proposals from the health minister would cost nothing for the government to implement and could even yield net revenues so it could easily be a policy that is kept in reserve by the government in order to distract attention from bad news elsewhere. In other words, it would be impossible to determine when such a policy would be proposed, if ever. In that event, we could easily waste resources in planning for such a contingency because there would be little or no warning as to when it will be put into effect.

Requirement 2 – share price

According to the efficient markets hypothesis, any share price movement will be rational in an economic sense if it is triggered by new information that has implications for future cash flows. Presumably, the stock market was aware of the possibility of a sugar tax, but the market would not know details such as the timing of any announcement or the details such as the planned rate of tax. The significant fall in the share price could be explained by concerns that the tax rate was higher than might have been expected or that the tax would be introduced sooner than had been expected.

Arguably, the share prices reflected the possibility of a sugar tax, allowing for doubt as to whether the tax would be levied and the timing of the change. The price reflected expectations, allowing for the possibility that the tax would not be charged or that the rate would be lower. The announcement itself would, therefore, have contained new information that could not have been available to the market in advance.

It would be a mistake to attribute the rapid recovery within hours of the price decrease to irrational behaviour. An efficient market requires information to reflect available information, but the announcement itself created a host of possibilities that would have to be evaluated. Market participants would have to contact sources in order to establish whether there was any further background information that could be obtained. That does not imply that the initial event was incorrectly priced, rather that the markets required time to fully explore the implications and look into other potential sources of information.

The share price could have fallen because investors might be concerned that some participants knew more than others. One strong possibility would be that the Minister had released an initial announcement with a view to adding further "bad news" later in the day in order to manage political implications, such as negative press comment.

When no bad news emerged, the markets could be reassured and might price the shares on the basis that no bad news would be forthcoming.

Share prices are driven by informed investors, who have the skills required to make sense of any news that becomes available. Such investors could make use of their skills to benefit from short-term speculative forces and gain at the expense of less skilled participants. The better informed investors might sell short when the news announcement was made, benefitting from their understanding of market psychology, and then close out their positions in the course of the day.

Exercise 2

Requirement 1 – digital strategy

Anthony's proposal goes beyond simply creating an app for consumers. It offers a means to protect revenues from the main products and to create additional revenue streams if the strategy proves successful. It could also create scope for the creation of new revenue streams that are related to the sale of existing products, but that exploit the data that the app will enable Fizz to gather.

The first question that we might ask is whether this is a suitable direction for Fizz. Fizz faces problems arising from the fact that its products can be unhealthy when consumed to excess. This app has the potential to raise consumers' awareness in a subtle way that encourages them to switch from unhealthy drinks to healthier products, including Fizz bottled water. Easing consumers away from high-calorie drinks in favour of healthier Fizz products could prove beneficial because of clear messages that traditional soft drinks are potentially harmful. In an ideal world, Fizz would probably benefit from ceasing the manufacture of unhealthy drinks so that it could focus on its range of sugar-free products. That would offer economies of scale in manufacturing and distribution.

Secondly, this strategy is feasible because Fizz's cans and bottles already have barcodes to enable them to be recognised by retailers' point of sale systems. It may prove moderately expensive to develop the app, but this should not be a major programming challenge and so the cost should be justified. The big question is whether consumers will download the app and use it. If it is promoted properly then consumers might view this as an attractive variation on social media. The operating costs should be minimal once the app is up and running. Even the discount vouchers will be affordable because they will be targeted at consumers whose custom is worth retaining.

Thirdly, the long-term acceptability of the app must be considered. Retailers will be interested in the data that will be collected, but only if the app reaches a sizeable group of consumers. If it succeeds in terms of penetration of the market then the app results will be of value in negotiating relationships with retailers and other manufacturers. It will effectively give Fizz a valuable data set that it can use to monetise its relationship with its consumers. The danger is that it will be easily replicated. It would not be difficult for other manufacturers to create their own apps, which might encroach on Fizz's market and dilute the value of the results. It may be more sustainable to develop the app in collaboration with other major drinks manufacturers.

Finally, Fizz may discover that a meaningful and constructive digital strategy requires more than an attractive app and it could suffer if it implements this idea without taking care. The app could create the impression that consumers' privacy is being invaded, particularly given that the app will generate feedback. If consumers get the impression that their data is being sold to retailers then that concern will be heightened. There is also a risk that the app will lead to an excessive reaction from consumers and that they will stop drinking Fizz altogether, rather than changing their lifestyle.

Requirement 2 – government concerns

Governments would generally prefer not to introduce laws that are potentially controversial and so might antagonise voters. The sugar tax is likely to prove unpopular with consumers whose preferred drinks will become more expensive. The best way to satisfy the government would be for Fizz to seek advice from the Ministry of Health when setting the parameters for different responses. The involvement of representatives from the Ministry would also make it easier for the government to justify relying at least in part on the app.

While the government may wish to rely on the app, it may prove politically impossible to do so. Politicians and other parties who have an interest in improving health will be suspicious of any actions taken by interested members of the industry that are claimed to be designed to tackle consumer safety. Fizz does not appear to have a genuine economic interest in reducing the sale of high-calorie drinks, otherwise it would have tackled this problem in a more drastic manner. The app appears to be an amusing activity for consumers, but the fact that it requires them to drink Fizz products in order to access it suggests that it could actually stimulate more sales of these drinks.

The government has already announced a sugar tax and it will appear weak if it is seen to withdraw that proposal in the face of industry lobbying. The development of the app may come too late to prevent the immediate action planned by the government. Realistically, the best that Fizz can hope to achieve is to actively persuade consumers to switch to sugar-free drinks so that it can minimise the impact of the sugar tax. This would be an opportunity to demonstrate a commitment to support the government's desire to improve health and could be helpful in influencing future government actions.

One compromise would be for Fizz to work with the government in the development of the app. The functions and coding could be left to the government's health department, so that there would be no doubt as to the value of the advice. Fizz might contribute by sponsoring the developments and helping with the distribution.

Exercise 3

Requirement 1 – controls and internal audit investigation

Fizz should grant each member of staff who works with app data a user name and password. The access permitted by these should be restricted to reflect the staff member's job. For example, access to app users' names and their email addresses might be restricted to customer service staff who have a need to deal directly with users and answer their queries. Other staff might be restricted to accessing non- personal details and summaries that they require to collate reports.

Data files should be accessible to staff with a need for access, but should not be downloadable or exportable. Files should be encrypted so that any copies cannot be opened by anybody who does not possess the key. That would make it impossible for staff to abuse files by downloading personal details and possibly selling them to third parties.

Fizz should take care when hiring staff to check their backgrounds and take up references. If the staff who have access to the files are competent and honest then they will be far less likely to abuse any access that they have in order to fulfil their duties. Staff induction and training should ensure that all staff are aware of their duty to respect customer privacy.

The app service is being provided by a new entity that was created as a subsidiary and staffed by new hires. Sending in an internal audit team would demonstrate the interest that Fizz's Board takes in the operation of that company. The message being sent to the staff through the involvement of the internal auditor could be sufficient justification for the investigation even if it discovered very little of value. It would ensure that staff are aware that the Board takes user privacy seriously and that any allegations will be investigated and dealt with.

The internal audit department is generally viewed as a service that supports the Board by checking compliance with laid down processes and procedures. The investigation would be a possible distraction from the internal plan, but the board has the right to decide on priorities and to redirect resources as it sees fit. The internal audit department would be able to respond quickly to any such request made by the Board.

The internal audit staff will be versatile and will be used to conducting ad hoc investigations. They will have the expertise to conduct any investigation that is set for them by the Board. They will also be trusted to report to the Board in confidence, with little risk of any adverse findings being leaked to regulators, the press or any other third parties.

Requirement 2 – ethics

Ignoring the external auditor's concerns would put Fizz in direct conflict with a number of fundamental principles of ethics.

Ignoring the concerns would be a breach of integrity because the protection of users' personal data would be taken for granted by the users themselves. They would expect Fizz to treat their data with respect and to ensure that it was not abused by anyone, including staff who might use it for their own purposes. Integrity requires Fizz to be straightforward and honest and so ignoring a potential breach of users' trust would be unacceptable.

Confidentiality is almost certainly a formal element of the agreement with users and Fizz has breached that by permitting unauthorised staff to gain access. The app will undoubtedly have a great deal of personal data that could be used to breach users' privacy. Fizz should take immediate steps to safeguard the users from any further breaches. Fizz should also take steps to warn users that they may be at risk because of the possibility that their contact details could be abused by unauthorised staff.

This is also a breach of the principle of professional behaviour, which requires Fizz to comply with all relevant laws and regulations. Most countries have very strict laws concerning the protection of personal data held by companies. Fizz is clearly in breach of those rules and management should check whether it has further legal obligations to attempt to rectify the default.

Requirement 3 – divestment

This venture is essentially Fizz's first digital strategy and it does provide an opportunity to learn from this and develop additional revenue sources. If the Board divests itself then it will be sending the message that Fizz does not wish to develop a meaningful digital strategy. This has been a high-profile activity and so the sale of the service could be viewed as a serious setback.

It may be difficult to sell the service for a meaningful sum, even though it has attracted 2m members. It would always be possible to develop a rival and to build up a significant following. In fact, social media has a history of users switching their loyalty to new platforms as they become available. Any potential buyer will consider the possible loss of members. The app could be worth more to Fizz because it would have a significant incentive to ensure that it remains current.

The primary purpose of the app was to demonstrate Fizz's commitment to encouraging users to consume healthy products. If the buyer agrees to continue to monitor users diets and to give the same encouragement then the app could fulfil Fizz's purpose, regardless of its new ownership. That could enable Fizz to create a more overtly commercial digital strategy that is designed to create revenues in a more explicit manner.

Feedback on the real exam and tips on answering tasks on the more technical aspects of F3

Chapter learning objectives

To understand how to improve the quality of answers when sitting a Strategic Case Study exam, and to understand how to answer the more technical aspects of F3.

1   Summary of exams to date

1.1   Examiner's feedback

After each exam sitting CIMA publish the exams, suggested answers, summary marking guides and an examiner's report that discusses all variants from that sitting.

While many students are producing high quality scripts in the time available, there are common themes that have arisen where students can improve. Here are the Examiner's reports from 2 exams set in 2019, the February and May sittings:

May 2019 – Examiner's report

Candidate performance

Overall, candidates performed reasonably well on some aspects of all the variants. However, there were a number of areas of concern relating to student performance in several other areas; this applies to all variants. The main weaknesses were that in several tasks, candidates failed to apply their knowledge directly to the scenario information and in some parts candidates just failed to answer what had been asked. On the positive side most candidates structured their answers well.

All answers must be applied to the case study and should bring in aspects of the pre-seen information as well as the information and exhibits in the unseen material. Most candidates did demonstrate application of knowledge which was good. Many candidates' answers lacked depth of development and therefore, although demonstrating a basic understanding and application of knowledge, they failed to accumulate sufficient marks due to not developing their answers sufficiently.

Candidates are reminded to carefully read each task requirement and only answer what has been asked. In addition, candidates are also reminded that theoretical answers are awarded very few marks.

Looking ahead to future examinations

Candidates should read the pre-seen material carefully and come into the examination understanding the industry and the company which will be the focus of the exam. This will help candidates formulate good answers that relate to the tasks they are given.

Candidates must manage their time well and make sure they do not run out of time on sections they know well.

Candidates must read the questions very carefully and answer what has been asked. Answers which are not applied to the case will not score high marks.

A good level of knowledge of the three strategic syllabi is necessary in order to do well in the exams. It is not enough to have knowledge of topics; candidates must be able to apply their knowledge to a variety of situations and show they have an in-depth knowledge of the subject matter.

February 2019 – Examiner's report

Candidate performance

Overall, candidates performed reasonably well on some aspects of all the variants. However, there were a number of areas of concern relating to student performance in several other areas; this applies to all variants. The main weaknesses were that in several tasks, candidates failed to apply their knowledge directly to the scenario information and in some parts candidates just failed to answer what had been asked. In many cases candidates quoted and described models but did not apply them to the case study; this approach does not gain marks.

All answers must be applied to the case study and should bring in aspects of the pre-seen information as well as the information and exhibits in the unseen material. Answers which are purely rote learning were quite common in some requirements and this approach is awarded very few marks. Many candidates' answers lacked depth of development and therefore, although demonstrating a basic understanding and application of knowledge, failed to accumulate sufficient marks due to insufficient development of answers.

Candidates are reminded to carefully read each task requirement and only answer what has been asked. In addition, candidates are also reminded that theoretical answers are awarded very few marks.

Looking ahead to future examinations

Candidates should read the pre-seen material carefully and come into the examination understanding the industry and the company which will be the focus of the exam. This will help candidates formulate good answers that relate to the tasks they are given.

Candidates must manage their time well and make sure they do not run out of time on sections they know well.

Candidates must read the questions very carefully and answer what has been asked. Answers which are not applied to the case will not score high marks.

A good level of knowledge of the three strategic syllabi is necessary in order to do well in the exams. It is not enough to have knowledge of topics; candidates must be able to apply their knowledge to a variety of situations and show they have an in-depth knowledge of the subject matter.

1.2   Lessons to be learnt from the above feedback

Whilst it might be argued that feedback has been mentioned from just 2 exam sittings and therefore represents a limited sample, the comments made above are recurrent themes in almost all examiner feedback reports. Students should look to take notice of all the relevant points made in the reports illustrated if they are to maximise their chances of success in this exam.

So, what are the learning points that we might take from the above reports?

- **Application of knowledge is critical**

  The examiners at Strategic Case Study are not testing how good your knowledge of the strategic syllabi is; you have already proved this by passing the three papers of E3, F3 and P3. Case study is a different exercise; what is now being demanded is whether you can *apply* this knowledge in a particular situation. Simply demonstrating rote learning, and therefore producing answers that look as though they may have come straight out of a study text, is not going to achieve sufficient marks for a pass.

- **Consider the pre-seen as well as the unseen material**

  The pre-seen material is deliberately released to students well in advance of the actual exam. This is to allow them to absorb the information that is contained within, to build up a bigger picture of the business that features within the case and the industry it operates in, and to perform some research on the industry itself. It should not then be ignored as soon as the examination begins! As well as containing the instructions, the unseen examination paper contains fresh materials that help to put the pre-seen into a more up to date context; students should therefore bear in mind how what they learnt from the pre-seen has now become better defined when they read the fresh materials.

- **Answers need depth of development**

  This means that often students do not develop their ideas sufficiently to gain good marks. They begin an answer by demonstrating good knowledge and even application of that knowledge, but do not then develop the ideas sufficiently.

  For example, say that a new competitor has just emerged, and is having an impact on the business that you work for. A candidate might suggest that, from a Porter's Five Forces analysis, the threat of new entrants would appear to be low, hence the new issue that there is a new competitive threat – at this point, the candidate is demonstrating knowledge. The candidate should then go on to talk about what this means for the business going forwards – will there be downwards pressure on profit margins? Are there likely to be added pressures from additional new entrants to the market? What unique selling points (USPs) can the business use to counteract the new threat? Is this likely to be an ongoing problem? What other advice would you give to the leadership team?

  It is only through proper development of ideas that students can hope to achieve good marks for insightful analysis.

- **Each task requirement must be read carefully**

  Sometimes it is possible to look at an instruction in an exam, think you have understood what is being asked of you, and then write a full and comprehensive answer (or so you believe!) only to realise subsequently that you have not scored as well as you might have hoped. This is most probably because you have failed to answer the question that was set. It may well be that you have produced an excellent response to a slightly different question, but the examiner cannot give you credit for this – you will only be judged on your ability to answer the precise instructions set to all candidates.

  It is therefore well worth investing time in reading through each task requirement very carefully, looking at the precise instructions that have been put forward. Think of the verbs that have been used, and refer back to the hierarchy of verbs that CIMA has used throughout your examination studies. Also, how many instructions are there? It may appear at first glance that you are being asked to do just one thing, but closer examination shows that there are actually two instructions in one.

  For example, if a task asks you to "Identify and evaluate", this will require you to pick up on matters that are relevant (identify) and then assess what the implications are for the business, possibly even concluding on the significance of the issue (evaluate).

- **Go into the exam understanding the industry**

  It is very important that you carry out some background research on the industry that features in your pre-seen. This will help you develop a much better appreciation of the broader issues facing the business that you work for, and may even point towards some of the themes that will feature in each of the five variants of the exam. Remember, the examiner has to derive inspiration from somewhere for writing exam questions – where better than the real world!

  For example, in the May 2019 exam Denby Healthcare (which was considered in chapter 2 of this text), an issue that was highlighted in the pre-seen was that of the local National Health Service using private hospital resources to ensure that patients did not have to wait any longer for treatment than the guidelines that the government had publicised. This then formed the outline of variant 2 of the exam.

  A student who had conducted industry research would have come across a wealth of information on this very topic. For example, consider the following:

  www.nhs.uk/common-health-questions/nhs-services-and-treatments/do-i-need-a-gp-referral-for-private-treatment/#

  https://www.bma.org.uk/-/media/files/pdfs/practical%20advice%20at%20work/ethics/interfaceguidanceethicsmay2009.pdf

www.nhs.uk/common-health-questions/nhs-services-and-treatments/if-i-pay-for-private-treatment-how-will-my-nhs-care-be-affected/

Great sources for information include the BBC, YouTube, online newspapers (the Guardian allows free access), and real world companies (for the Denby Healthcare case, it would have served students well to look at organisations such as BUPA, Nuffield Healthcare, and the Spire, as well as other organisations). Naturally, Google is also very useful.

- **Manage time well**

  It is interesting to note that time management overall does not appear to be a problem in Case Study; 3 hours would seem perfectly sufficient to answer the instructions that are set. However, the examiner sees evidence of students coming across a task that they are clearly confident with, and then spending far too long on creating an answer that is excessive.

  Success in case study is about making a decent attempt at **all** of the instructions set; you will find it very difficult to pass through providing a detailed answer to one instruction, and only a very brief or shallow answer to another. Use the time guidance given on the opening screen of the exam to determine how long you should spend on each instruction, and stick to it.

  For example, in the previous chapter, the prototype exam Paper for Fizz contained the following information on the first screen:

Section (task)	Time for section (minutes)	Number of answer screens	Number of sub-tasks	% time to spend on each sub-task
1	60	1	2	(a) 55% (b) 45%
2	60	1	2	(a) 55% (b) 45%
3	60	1	3	(a) 60% (b) 20% (c) 20%

  This would therefore mean that, for task 1 which has a total of 60 minutes allocated to it, candidates should spend 55% of that time on sub-task a), and 45% on sub-task b). This means no more than 33 minutes on the first sub-task and the rest on the second. The examiner will be thinking about the amount of content expected for each sub-task and will therefore provide such guidance accordingly. Ignoring such advice is high risk!

2 Answering more technical aspects of F3

2.1 Introduction

In the November 2018 report, the examiner made the following comment:

"There are always F pillar questions, and they always by far the weakest answers."

This is not the only occasion that such a comment has been made in the Examiner's report. It should therefore be asked what students can do to improve in such requirements. In the next section we consider an example of such a task from the May 2019 exam.

You may wish to revisit chapter 2 at this point to refresh your memory on what the Denby Healthcare case involved.

2.2 Variant 1, task 1

The second instruction to this task would have addressed core activity 3 of the syllabus, Recommend financing strategies, with the associated assessment outcome of "I can recommend suitable sources of finance"

Scenario

- Denby would look to establish specialist 'Denby Sports Injury Centres' at its hospitals

- It would need to raise $130 million of fresh finance to fund this.

The requirement

"Would it be irresponsible for Denby's Board to borrow the K$130 million required for this purpose?"

Possible answer approach/structure

As mentioned earlier, it is vital that students correctly interpret the instruction that is given. It would be easy to misinterpret this task if looked at only briefly; for example, it could be interpreted as "How might Denby's Board raise the K$130 million required for this purpose?"

That is not what the question is asking!

If a student had interpreted the requirement in this way, then a logical structure would have been:

1   Talk about equity finance

- Start with a general explanation of how equity might be raised – retained earnings, squeezing working capital, rights issue, new equity issue.

- Then perhaps comment on the pros and cons of equity finance – how it might affect control for shareholders, the greater flexibility it can present to cash flows (no obligation to pay a dividend), the different levels of cost associated with each source, etc.

2   Talk about debt finance

- Then move on to talk about debt, and how this might be raised – a term loan, leasing or perhaps debentures.

- Next, comment on the pros and cons of debt finance – the tax shield on interest, the lower cost to the company compared to equity, the obligation to pay interest each year, etc.

3   Conclusion.

- Finally, conclude on which source is preferable for Denby Healthcare.

Unfortunately, the above approach would have been guilty of many of the criticisms mentioned when reviewing the examiner's reports at the start of this chapter. It began badly when the student failed to answer the question actually set, and soon turned into a general discussion of sources of finance as opposed to one that is tailored to Denby Healthcare itself.

Suggested answer approach/structure

Again, correct interpretation of the task is vital. What is the question asking students to do?

It is asking if raising the finance required via debt is 'irresponsible'. This means is it an appropriate way to raise the finance, and what impact might it have on the company? It is not asking for a detailed examination of equity.

A suggested structure might therefore be:

1   Talk about the impact on financial gearing

- Look at the current gearing level of Denby Healthcare, and consider how a further K$130 million of debt would affect this. Would it make the financial gearing levels excessive? How might key stakeholders, such as shareholders, react?

- You could also look at the statement of profit and loss; how might the extra debt impact on a key ratio such as interest cover? Would the company's overall profitability be put at risk with extra interest payable obligations?

2   Talk about what Denby would have to pay to secure the debt

- What is likely to be a lender's required rate of return? Does Denby have assets to offer as security to reduce the risk to the lender, thereby reducing the rate of interest payable on the debt?

3   Conclusion.

- After considering the above, is taking on the finance in the form of debt 'irresponsible'? Might equity be a better proposal? If so, justify **briefly** such a comment.

Examiner's comments

The question essentially raised two related issues. Borrowing to fund this project will increase gearing. That raises questions about whether the gearing ratio is likely to be raised beyond acceptable limits. Better candidates should have recognised that gearing will increase, but not to the extent that there is a categorical argument that it has become excessive.

The increase in gearing should have been considered against the possibility that the new venture will have an adverse effect on operating profit. It should always be recognised that high gearing is a problem because it intensifies the effect of volatility in operating profit on the profit for the year. If there is no volatility in operating profit then gearing is much less of an issue.

Candidates might also have considered whether lenders would be prepared to accept Denby's assets as security. They may have limited resale value, if a lender could accept the bad publicity associated with foreclosing on a hospital and removing potentially life-saving equipment. This question was done quite well by many candidates with many discussing gearing well. Weaker candidates did not mention gearing at all. Few candidates mentioned the issue of using assets as security which was disappointing. Some candidates decided to say that equity would be better and gave a whole answer on equity, which did not gain high marks.

2.3 Variant 2, task 3

The third instruction to this task would have addressed core activity 3 of the syllabus, Recommend financing strategies, with the associated assessment outcome of "I can recommend dividend policy."

Scenario

- Denby would look to buy 4 hospitals in need of refurbishment to bring them up to acceptable standard. The cost of these hospitals would be a nominal K$1

- Denby would then invest K$250 million in refurbishment.

- This would result in the new hospitals being referred National Health Service patients exclusively, and the whole Denby Group being treated as a preferred supplier.

- If Denby did not proceed with this proposal, it could use some of its considerable cash reserves to pay a significant dividend to shareholders.

The requirement

"How would the payment of a significant dividend affect shareholder wealth?"

Suggested answer approach/structure

Once again, it is important to recognise that this question is not asking you to recite everything you know about dividend policy; the trap you could easily fall into is to write about Modigliani and Miller's ideas compared to the traditional viewpoint, and then conclude with some practical suggestions.

Focus on the instruction: "How would the payment of a significant dividend affect shareholder wealth?"

To paraphrase the instruction, in what ways might paying a significant dividend increase shareholder wealth, and in what ways might it reduce it?

A suggested structure is therefore:

1   Talk about shareholder wealth

- Returns to shareholders from equity investments come in two forms – a dividend income stream, and capital gain in the value of their investment.

- A significant dividend may certainly have a positive effect on shareholder wealth in the short term – more return is being received than anticipated.

2   Talk about impact on share price

- How will the market react to the payment of a large dividend? It might perceive that the increased level will be typical of the future, and so a short term increase results; if the new level cannot be maintained in future, it will probably fall again. This results in share price volatility, which shareholders typically do not like.

- Shareholders might feel that a company such as Denby needs to keep investing to fund future growth, and that paying a significant dividend might reduce such possibilities. In this case, the share price is likely to fall.

3   Other matters

- Investors will have different preferences on how wealth is increased, depending on their tax position; some investors may prefer income, others capital gain.

- Much will depend on how news of the dividend is released to the market. If it is clearly explained that this is a one-off extra payment, the share price is likely to remain stable.

Examiner's comments

This requirement was answered reasonably well by candidates, many of whom were able to present a sound discussion of the implications of paying a large dividend to its shareholders. Good answers also included points relating to the tax considerations of shareholders.

Weaker answers were those that merely considered that the markets may be misled as to the level of future dividends.

2.4 Variant 5, task 2

The second instruction to this task would have addressed core activity 3 of the syllabus, Recommend financing strategies, with the associated assessment outcome of "I can recommend dividend policy."

Scenario

- Denby would look to buy BNC, a nursing college in the country of Bordia. Acquiring BNC could ensure that Denby has a reliable source of competent nurses.

- BNC is still owned by its founders, and is unquoted. Denby has many current nurses that were trained at BNC on its three year programme.

- BNC receives no state funding; its income is earned solely from fees paid by nurses for courses.

- BNC barely breaks even due to the high cost of running nursing degrees.

The requirement

"What basis should we use to determine the value of BNC to Denby?"

Suggested answer approach/structure

This question is not asking you to recite everything you know about valuation techniques. It is asking you to apply your knowledge of such matters to this specific circumstance. You should therefore ask yourself what techniques might be relevant here.

You might start by asking yourself what techniques exist. You will probably consider the following:

- Net assets approach

- Dividend based

- Use of a price/earnings (P/E) ratio

- Discounted future cash flows

A suggested structure is therefore:

1   Introduce valuation techniques, and dismiss those likely to be irrelevant

- As BNC is barely breaking even, it is unlikely to be paying dividends, and so the dividend valuation model is not relevant. Also, this is more useful for valuing a minority stake.

- Similarly, if there is little profit, using a P/E multiple will result in a very low number.

- This therefore leaves the net assets approach and discounted future cash flows as potentially relevant.

2   Talk about the net assets approach

- What are the likely assets of BNC? Possibly premises and training equipment, which gives a tangible value, but the largest asset of a training organisation is surely the staff (and possibly the business' reputation) – neither of these will be on the balance sheet, and so adjustment would need to be made.

- Net assets could also indicate the maximum Denby should be prepared to pay, as this represents the opportunity cost of acquisition (Denby could, alternatively, set up a business like BNC from scratch).

3   Talk about discounted cash flows

- Whilst profits might be low, BNC may still generate positive cash flows (low profits could be due to issues such as impairments). This would suggest BNC has some value.

- Future cash flows should incorporate synergies that result from the acquisition e.g. Denby saving on recruitment fees.

4   Conclusion

- Using both measures will give Denby a range of values upon which to base a negotiation with the current owners of BNC.

Examiner's comments

Many answers were a little weak as they failed to use the information given in the scenario. Many candidates identified the weakness of the financial performance of BNC and valued the business very simply as future cash flows. However, there were some excellent response to this requirement.